Making Your Phone Ring with Internet Marketing
for Window Covering Companies

Making Your Phone Ring With Internet Marketing
for Window Covering Companies

Second Edition

Welton Hong

Founder of Ring Ring Marketing®
ringringmarketing.com

Thanks to my parents Shunhua and Sumei for their guidance, my wife Ihsuan for just about everything, and to my siblings William and Jennifer who make it all worthwhile.

CONTENTS

FOREWORD TO THE NEW EDITION

Thank you for taking the time to check out the brand-new second edition of my book *Making Your Phone Ring with Internet Marketing for Window Covering Companies*.

Over the last few years, few things have been as gratifying to me as the opportunity to educate home improvement professionals on all the new marketing techniques available in the digital age.

One inescapable truth about marketing in today's technologically advanced era is that things change quickly. In the eighties, nineties, and even early 2000s, you could count on the same marketing and advertising techniques to produce consistent results year after year.

That's no longer the case. Thanks to enormous technological advances, Americans today interact with their world in massively different ways, and the means by which they do evolve substantially every year. Sometimes, the process is even faster than that!

That's why I felt it was so important to create a fully updated edition of this comprehensive book about marketing for window covering pros. A *ton* has changed since 2013, and I want to make sure you completely understand the landscape as head into 2020.

Many of the tools and techniques I referenced in the previous edition still work well today, but now there are several different ways to leverage them for a maximum return on investment.

There are also some new weapons for your arsenal, and they'll come in handy as you face challenges from increasingly tech-savvy competitors.

It's critical that you take advantage of the many opportunities available to you online. In virtually every region of the United States, there's fertile digital ground you can seize before your competitors do.

It's like the Wild West. You need to get out there and plant your flag before your competitors do!

If you enjoyed the 2013 edition of this book, I hope you'll make a point of thoroughly reading this new edition. While you're recognize some original material that remains foundational to a successful marketing strategy, you'll also discover a lot of new (and very important) information.

And if this is your first time reading my book on window covering marketing, welcome! I know you'll come away with a much better understanding of how your window treatment company can profit from the techniques detailed within.

~ Welton Hong

INTRODUCTION:
The Yellow Pages is history.
It's time to move forward.

Yes, it's true.

The Yellow Pages is history.

(You'll note that I said the Yellow Pages is history, as opposed to the Yellow Pages **are** *history. Yes, I know it sounds weird. Blame whoever gave a plural name to a singular directory.)*

What you just read above is how I began the introduction to the first edition of this book (in 2013).

As we head into the bold new world of 2020, it's still there — for a good reason:

It's all still true. Honestly, it's truer than ever.

I made the point about the Yellow Pages to hammer home a critical fact: You can't count on old-school print directories anymore to market your window covering business.

Does that mean you'll never get a call from a Yellow Pages listing and/or an ad? Of course not. As you know, it still happens now and then. We all have older relatives who instinctively reach for that massive book whenever they need a local business.

And that's fine. Frankly, if you still get a handful of calls every year from the Yellow Pages, that might well be enough return on investment to keep with it.

In my experience, *any marketing method that returns a positive ROI or at least breaks even* is worth continuing.

To succeed in business, you must maximize your revenue. To accomplish that, you must do what other businesses do:

You must *multiply your capital*.

That means intelligently *reinvesting your capital* in marketing methods that consistently produce greater revenue. Many techniques I detail in this book achieve exactly that result.

And while digital marketing is my chief area of expertise, I remain a fan of any offline marketing effort that generates revenue for your home improvement company.

➔ That could be the print Yellow Pages.

➔ It could be a local church directory.

➔ It could be a direct mail campaign.

Depending on the particulars of your area, it could even be billboards, bus bench advertising—you name it.

If it's working for you, do it.

You don't have to drop all the "old-school" methods just because digital has taken over so much of how we do business today.

But…

(You knew there was going to be a *but*, right?)

But…the reality is that more and more print directories go straight into recycling bins as we close out 2020. Heck, they were already starting to be on their way out six years ago, when I wrote the first edition of this book.

Today, everyone has a smartphone. Most Americans have a smartphone and a tablet. And many also have other devices to conveniently access the internet 24/7.

The 2018 holiday season brought American households a ton of smart speakers, incredibly user-friendly devices that sit on counters and tablets. You can get information just by calling out to Google or Alexa or Siri (or Amazon for retail needs).

Which means that if a homeowner has an immediate need for information on window treatments, all they need to do is call out to the speaker for a local recommendation.

It's that easy now. You don't even have to get out of your chair and fish out the Yellow Pages. You can place a call to a home improvement company without even grabbing your phone.

The window covering businesses getting those calls? They're the ones that *optimized* their businesses for that purpose. Which is a basic element of digital marketing.

You might be thinking that most homeowners who contact you probably still aren't getting information through a smart speaker. That's somewhat true. It will be another year or two until that technology reaches more widespread adoption.

But you *do* know many that will go straight to the internet for information. That's been the trend for years now, and again — yes, you'll hear this a lot — it's especially true as we rapidly close in on 2020.

They might go to a desktop computer to do a search. They might also reach for a convenient tablet. And it's entirely possible that they'll simply pick up their phone. Why not? They can simply use their voice to do a search on their phone (much like a smart speaker). Or they might just type in their search.

Either way, simply asking for "local window treatment business" or "window covering business near me" or even just "window fashions" — search engines such as

Google know where you are, after all, and just search locally anyway — will immediately pull up local listings.

If you've done your due diligence with search engine optimization (SEO), you'll be at the top of those listings. (Or at least *near* the top, if you're in an especially competitive area.) If you haven't, you won't get those calls.

Of course, the other obvious benefit to a smartphone is that it's entirely portable. You always have the internet right at your fingertips, no matter where you are or what time it is.

So if you're away from home — even thousands of miles away — and you suddenly find your home needing window covering services due to weather damage, it's no problem at all. You just reach for your phone.

You can access a business in a matter of seconds.

Thanks to click-to-call technology, you can be *on the phone with a window covering professional with a single tap*.

That's how easy it is. And a homeowner will contact your business that way — *if* you've optimized for mobile.

If you haven't, some other local window treatment company is getting that call.

I run a pay-for-results business. Here's what that means: **If you doesn't make money, I don't make money**. At Ring Ring Marketing, I've always operated with the mindset that *your success is our success*.

I wouldn't have it any other way. That's how I was raised. I'm not going to accept your money if I can't take that investment and turn it into significant revenue generation for your business.

That's why RRM has a 100 percent money-back guarantee for a full 60 days. My business *depends* on the window covering companies I partner with making money.

So I can't afford to beat around the bush. I have to be honest about challenges facing the industry. I can't pretend you have all the time in the world to get around to accepting the digital revolution and prioritizing online marketing for your business.

That's why I have to cut to the chase:

Things are changing incredibly rapidly right now, and if you *don't act very soon, you'll be left behind.*

The change was on the horizon when personal computers became standard in people's homes. But the big turn, the first one, occurred when a 24/7 internet connection became more common than not.

That's when people realized they could just as easily jump on their computers and look up listings for local businesses without breaking out the phone book. And as more and more businesses invested in websites and listings on Google and similar sites, specific information about those businesses became available.

Businesses could provide much more information (at no extra cost) on their sites and listings than they ever could in a Yellow Pages listing or ad.

Customer reviews, hours of business, recent testimonials — all of that and more was available to potential customers whenever they liked.

That was the status quo for a while, but another big sea change occurred over just the past decade with two great technological innovations: smartphones and tablets.

It's one thing to be able to access information from around the world in the comfort of your home. It's something else entirely to have that information available in the palm of your hand, 24 hours a day, no matter where you are: at the coffee shop, in the park, in your car.

As I write this in 2020, smartphones are now far more powerful than a top-of-the-line personal computer used to be. The same is true of tablets. And with increases in speed and download power, it's now incredibly easy for someone with only the most basic understanding of technology to access all this information in seconds.

Connecting with homeowners who need your services is increasingly becoming an online process. That's just the reality in 2020, when many people have moved on from print advertising and now exclusively determine their service providers by going online.

And while that might sound like a purely generational thing ("only Generation Z or maybe millennials do that"), it's not true.

Generation X has shown *no* allegiance to print advertising in this digital age. And in 2020, even many baby boomers are more likely to get information from their desktop computers or (even more likely) tablets and smartphones than from the Yellow Pages, or a newspaper (many of which are also on the brink of extinction), or any other print product.

That's how much things have changed.

A few years ago, many of the websites you pulled up on your smartphone would be hard to read or even unintelligible, because those sites had been created to be viewed on a large computer monitor.

That's no longer the case. The most successful sites now appear in mobile versions that look perfectly fine on everything from a tablet to even a small smartphone.

(Yours must be too, which I'll cover later when we talk about having a **mobile-friendly website**.)

The key to this transition: No longer are only the young or the especially tech-savvy looking for product or service information on their phones or tablets.

Now, *everyone*, from a preteen to a great-grand-mother, can do this quickly and easily. That's how far the technology has improved in a short time.

That's why the print Yellow Pages are virtually extinct now, and types of print advertising from newspaper ads to magazines are continuing to plummet in reach and effectiveness.

In 2020, the term "marketing" means, for the most part, "internet marketing."

Yes, some offline methods still work — and as I noted before, many are worth trying — but if you're not marketing your business on the internet in today's world, you're invisible to a huge swath of potential customers.

As the owner of a window treatment business, you have a number of potential marketing outlets available to you, but in today's digital age, one thing is irrefutable:

If you're not promoting yourself online, you're losing critical exposure with every month that passes.

The transition from print to digital has affected members of every generation, including those who grew up without 24/7 internet or even household personal computers.

Even Americans who are well into their retirement years have adapted to the notion of researching local business services digitally.

A recent survey showed that 90 percent of respondents felt that advertising in the Yellow Pages was ineffective.

While it's certainly true that some people discover local home improvement services through traditional word of mouth and print/radio ads, that's less the case as we progress further into the 21st century.

Our population has become increasingly transient. A half-century ago, many people still lived their entire lives in the same town. That's far rarer today.

Instead, many go straight to Google (or, much less often, Yahoo or Bing) and do a search. It's free and convenient — the internet is at our fingertips 24 hours a day — so why not?

You can think of the evolution from print marketing to internet marketing as having a physical business that for many years was situated along a major road through your town.

Let's say that for many years, people saw your window treatment company's physical location and inquired about services because they couldn't miss you. Your building is there, your sign is there, and you're convenient to acccss.

Let's extend the hypothetical situation: A major U.S. highway is built in your town, just a few blocks from your store. Suddenly all the traffic comes down *that* highway, not the formerly major street where your store still resides. No one travels past you anymore.

You might have a great business, but *no one knows you're there*.

You might even be *much better* than your competitors now situated along the U.S. highway, but it doesn't matter, because your competitors are the "storefronts" people *actually see*. They're convenient to access. Those businesses are *where the people are*.

Today, ***the internet is where the people are***. And you get their attention by having a website that's optimized to be found when people are looking for what you do, specifically in your local market.

You get their attention by having comprehensive listings for your window treatment business on Google and other major internet sites.

You get their attention by promoting your business on Facebook, Twitter, and other social media sites. It has to be done creatively, of course, but it can be done.

That might all sound like a lot, but it really isn't. If you need a hand with the technical issues, qualified internet marketing experts can handle those matters, letting you focus on what you do well: providing exceptional window covering services to homeowners.

The key is to understand that as we approach 2020, online marketing is no longer just a *facet* of your marketing plan.

It is the foundation of your marketing plan.

Business owners who ignore this fact will find themselves being ignored as we continue into this digital age.

In the rest of this book, I'll go over the basics. I'll explain how an online marketing professional can help you present your services to potential customers and ensure excellent word of mouth for referrals.

I'll show you how a range of tools — many of them quite simple and affordable — can expand the reach of your business exponentially.

No matter what, the key thing I hope you'll understand is that today, every month that goes by without actively promoting your window treatment business online is a massive waste of potential. The playing field keeps changing all the time, and it's incredibly easy to get left behind.

The good news is this: If you act soon and get your "online house" in order, you won't just be benefitting from everything that a well-designed internet marketing campaign can do for you.

You'll also have a massive advantage on local competitors who have been slower to adapt to the new online marketing world.

You will be recording in digital while they're still recording in analog. You'll be transmitting in high-definition while they're still using rabbit ears. You'll be operating in the present while they're still operating in the past. And that's a *gigantic* advantage in today's business world.

You want to be the window covering business holding that advantage, not the one watching from the sidelines.

I'm here to show you how to do it.

Section 1:

Lead Generation

CHAPTER 1
Search Engine Marketing (SEM)

I'm going to presume your home improvement company has a website, and thus you have at least some idea of what **search engine marketing** (SEM) entails.

Without a website, a business might as well not have a front door or a phone. It's absolutely integral.

(If you didn't have at least some type of window covering website, let's be honest, you probably wouldn't be reading this book.)

Regardless, let's go over the basics of SEM. In a nutshell, it's an umbrella term for a variety of tools that provide your site the *best possible visibility* online given certain factors.

In other words, you're obviously not competing for visibility against every other site in the world. No matter what you do, you're not going to be more visible than Amazon for retail goods or more visible than iTunes more music sales.

Today, you'll most often hear "SEM" as referring to paid digital advertising, such as Google Ads, whereas "SEO" is reserved for organic search. But for our purposes here, we'll consider SEM to broadly cover all of the above.

In SEM, you want your site to be more visible than the sites of local competitors in your industry. As a local business, that means optimizing your site (and your marketing efforts) to rank higher in search engine results pages (SERPs) than other window covering service providers in your market and in outlying areas you serve.

These days, online search is extremely specialized. Certain strategies and tools let you put your best foot forward in a particular area and market.

Some of these tools essentially require no advertising dollars; by optimizing your site with particular keywords and types of content, the site will organically rank well in your market and area.

Other tools require dipping into your marketing budget, such as letting you bid on particular keywords that people who are looking for your type of service will be using when they search.

For your business, this likely would include various forms of keyword phrases including targeted keywords that should include your city and state, along with the words *window treatments, window coverings, window fashions, window blinds, window shutters, window shades,* etc.

A successful internet marketing plan typically combines both approaches, one that balances the initiatives of organic SEO and paid advertising (which is now most often referred to specifically as SEM).

In this chapter, I'll cover the basics of **pay-per-click advertising** (PPC), **local search optimization**, and **search engine optimization** (SEO).

Pay-Per-Click Advertising (PPC)

Pay-per-click (PPC) is an umbrella term for several types of advertising, such as sponsored listings, paid search, partner ads, or sponsored links — with one thing in common:

In each type, you pay for the ad only when a user clicks it and is forwarded to your website (or whatever destination page you set up).

Most often, you'll find PPC ads atop pages when you do online searches — you'll recall those pages are called SERPs, or search engine results pages.

Google remains the dominating industry leader in search, with about *90 percent* of the organic search market share and about *80 percent* of the search ad market share as of early 2020. (Yes, it's *that* dominant.)

Its PPC function is an aspect of Google Ads, the venture that provides Google the vast majority of its revenue.

(A couple of quick notes: Google's parent company is technically "Alphabet," which is essentially just a renaming of its corporate entity. That occurred in fall 2015. Until summer 2018, Google Ads was known as "Google AdWords," which is what many people still call it out of habit, but it technically now goes by the simpler name.)

One of the coolest things about PPC ads is that they don't appear until someone completes a search.

Because they're dynamic, the ads that appear following the search will be relevant to whatever the user is searching for. The ads are, by definition, *targeting an interested party.*

The other obvious benefit is that the ad doesn't cost you a penny simply for appearing: *You only pay when it gets clicked*, sending the user to your page and providing an opportunity to convert the visitor into a client.

Creating a PPC account can differ slightly depending on the platform (an internet marketing professional can explain the process and handle it for you). But here's the general game plan:

First, you'll create a PPC account with the particular platform, a simple enough process. Next, you'll create campaigns and ad groups.

The campaign part is where you determine options such as the geography of the market you wish to reach. Because your business relies on local homeowners, for example, you'll obviously want local targeting.

That's how localized search and advertising is these days: You can set it up so only people in your city, county, or state (depending on your preferences) see your ads and thus click on them.

The ad groups comprise your advertisements and keyword lists. An internet marketing professional can help you determine whether there are any other specific terms people will be searching for when they want to find a business that provides your particular services.

Remember that despite the name, *a keyword isn't necessarily just a single word*; it's very often a phrase. When a keyword phrase comprises more than one word (typically three or more), it's commonly called a **long-tail keyword**. You'll incorporate these keywords in the ads you run in your campaign.

The particular search engine for that campaign will determine how well the advertiser's campaigns and key-words match the user's particular search, and it will display the ads if there's a close match.

A few other factors determine whether your ad will show up. Every search engine has an algorithm that considers these factors and employs them with each search. These factors include:

- How closely do the keywords in the list match the actual search?
- Does the advertisement itself include a mention of what the user is looking for?

- Does the ad forward the user to a landing page selling the service the user wants?

- How much are you willing to pay for a user searching for these terms to see your ad (and hopefully click through to it)?

The final point — the actual amount of your bid — determines not only how much you'll pay, but also *how prominently* your ad is displayed on the page.

The specifics of each search engine's algorithm are not made public for a sound reason: It keeps less legitimate advertisers from gaming the system, crafting ads that exist only to get clicks without actually providing the user anything useful.

Google, in particular, has tweaked its algorithms substantially over the years to reward websites and advertisers who are legitimately providing good information and selling useful services and products. This is happening not only in PPC but in search engine rankings; we'll talk about this some more later.

The thing to remember is this: If you provide good content on your website/landing page and craft good PPC ads to market your window treatment business, you'll be rewarded.

If your sites and ads are intended to mislead people into clicking through just to increase site traffic, you're taking a chance on being penalized by search providers, particularly Google.

This is one of the most common **black-hat** tactics. Anything you see referred to as "black hat" is a nefarious attempt to game the system. I can assure you, **you**

never want to employ black-hat tactics. No truly reputable marketing company ever does.

If Google or other search engines catch you trying to game the system, your entire digital presence could be massively penalized. It's absolutely not worth the risk.

Instead, only work with companies who employ **white-hat** techniques. As you've surely inferred, that means doing things the right way. (Which we would *hope* every home improvement business would do.)

Whatever short-term benefits a business might receive from black-hat tactics will be far outweighed by the massive damage it can do when Google sniffs it out. And Google *will* sniff it out: It's like the IRS — just much faster and smarter.

Whether PPC is a valuable investment for your window treatment business depends on several considerations. A big one is whether your website/landing page typically shows up near the top of the results when people are searching for the window covering services you provide in your area.

As anyone can tell you, many people don't bother searching past the first page of SERPs. (Think about it: How often do you continue to Page 2 or 3 after doing a Google search?)

Being ranked on that first page is critical. If you're not ranked there for whatever reason — your site isn't sufficiently optimized for search engines, or you're in a highly competitive market — you're virtually invisible even if you're near the top of the listings on Page 2.

If you're even deeper in the SERPs, you really *are* invisible. Most searchers, if they don't find what they're looking for by Page 2, will just try a new search with some different keywords.

A PPC ad lets you essentially jump ahead of the SERP organic listings, putting your site/landing page right out front. Granted, this comes at a price, and some searchers can be reluctant to click on an ad as opposed to a search result *per se* — but they become more comfortable with search ads every single year.

PPC remains an *extremely effective tool* for many reasons. It provides a lot of control and is highly customizable. You only pay if the ad is clicked.

Pay-per-click advertising also makes it easy to get extremely accurate statistics on whether your ad is effective, unlike most traditional types of advertising.

Best of all, if your home improvement company needs to increase service contracts rapidly, PPC is the perfect tool for the job. PPC ads are highly visible, and they're especially well displayed on mobile devices.

Smartphone users can call your firm with a single click on a mobile PPC ad. And that's one of the biggest keys to digital marketing success: *Make it easy for a potential customer to contact you.*

Whether you get the call or a competing home improvement company does often come down to simply which one put up fewer obstacles for the searcher. When you make it easy, you get the call.

The analytics of PPC ads let you know which keywords people used to find your page, so you can tweak your keywords depending on which ones worked well (or poorly).

You'll know how many people departed a page on your site immediately after reaching it (known as your **bounce rate**) — and how many stuck around.

One of the biggest benefits of PPC (aka paid search) advertising is that it *bridges the time gap* between SEO improvements to your website and when they're recognized by Google.

Improving your organic SEO (the right way) goes a long way toward elevating your search rankings for people searching for window fashion services in your area.

However, Google only "crawls" your site (more on that later) occasionally, so it won't know immediately that you should be ranked high on the first page of results.

By comparison, PPC ads post almost immediately, letting you get your name right out front while you're waiting on Google to review your window covering site and increase your organic ranking.

Some other benefits to PPC advertising to home in on the right demographics and target the best leads:

Geography: This is a key factor in ensuring that you're targeting the most qualified leads. Analytical information lets you tweak the geography of your ads to concentrate on markets where they're doing well (and lets you pull them from markets where you're not garnering interest).

Similarly, one of the most useful aspects of PPC advertising is that you can target potential customers in very specific geographic areas.

For example, a PPC ad can be set to only appear *within a set radius* of a business's physical location. This is a great option for a window treatment company, obviously, because homeowners use a local provider.

In addition to radius, PPC ads can be set to run only in particular ZIP codes or cities. Whatever exact areas you wish to target, your PPC ads can be focused entirely on them.

If you wish to cast a broader net, no problem. Unlike physical media such as the Yellow Pages, it costs *nothing extra* to target multiple cities.

You're not paying five or six times as much to run an ad in five or six cities — *one price fits all*. Thus the cost per lead is far less expensive than it would be with traditional media.

Day parting: As with geographical targeting, PPC ads can be set up to run only during the times of the day or week you want them to run.

Day	Time period	Midnight	4:00 AM	8:00 AM	Noon	4:00 PM	8:00 PM
Monday	07:00 AM - 07:00 PM						
Tuesday	07:00 AM - 05:00 PM						
Wednesday	Running all day						
Thursday	Running all day						
Friday	Noon - 04:00 PM						
Saturday	Running all day						
Sunday	Running all day						

Controlling lead flow: The scheduling of PPC ads can be easily modified to increase traffic. Google charges based on a daily budget.

Let's say you typically spend $30 per day, but there's a period where you need to increase your new business flow and have some room in your budget. You can increase it to $50 for more coverage.

On the other hand, let's say your window treatment company is already very busy at the present time. You could knock down your PPC ad budget to $15 for a while to save some money and ensure you don't get overwhelmed. (If you're busy already, why spend money on ads?)

And if you're literally *overwhelmed* with business at a particular time — a good problem to have, but a challenge nonetheless — you can even *pause your ads* for whatever time frame you determine.

This also comes in handy if your business is closed for a period of time or tends to be busier and/or slower in particular seasons — which obviously is true of window covering businesses in most areas.

In this sense, running PPC ads is like turning the knob on a faucet: You can open it up to flow freely, turn it down to a trickle, or turn it off entirely for a while, all dependent on your needs at the time.

Instant traffic: As I noted before, PPC ads let you be seen on the first page of search results almost immediately. *You're paying for the opportunity to jump to the front of the pack.*

This makes PPC a powerful tool for seeing a very fast return on an online marketing campaign. When used in tandem with organic SEO and local optimization strategies, you will see your traffic soar and watch it continue climbing in both the short and long term.

PPC ads are never static: Anything can be tweaked, adjusted, or swapped out at any time. With print media, you're stuck with the same print ad for a long time. In the case of the Yellow Pages, you're stuck with it for an *entire year*.

If there are changes in your business — you add a location, you change the geographical area you're targeting, you revise your services in some way — the Yellow Pages ad will still have all the old information until it's time for a new edition of the print directory.

PPC ads let you change the content on the fly. If you want to make a change for a short time to increase business, such as a reduced cost for particular window covering products or services, you can have the new ad appearing "live" to searchers in only a day or two.

Trying lots of variations: With a typical print ad, you come up with terms and phrasing you think will work best, cross your fingers, and hope it does the job.

PPC advertising lets you try out many different variations of ads catered to the keywords you want. You literally could have hundreds or even thousands of different variations employed at the same time.

(To keep things easy to manage, you'll likely only want to employ a handful of keywords, but you get the idea.)

This also allows for **split testing** of the different choices, letting you know quickly which ads have the most impact and which are less successful.

Additionally, when you have several ads running simultaneously with differently worded long-tail keywords, the ads people see will typically match up with the terms they're specifically searching for.

If they search for "new shades," they'll get the ad with *that* focus. If they search for "replacement blinds," they'll get the ad with *that* focus. Same with "blackout curtains" or "window treatments for kids' rooms," etc.

This is another way in which PPC advertising beats out print, because in something such as the Yellow Pages, you have to determine which sections you want to be listed in and place ads in *all* of them.

Excellent branding tool: If improving brand awareness is a critical concern for your window treatment company, PPC is an effective tool. If people click on your ad, that's great: They're coming to your website to consider your services. If they don't, you're *still getting exposure* to lots of people searching for what you provide, improving your brand awareness.

Note: Now, I know that terms such as "brand awareness" can sound strange to some window covering professionals. You *sell* brands. Your business is not a brand itself. Right? Well…not entirely.

You actually are a brand. Accept it and incorporate it into your marketing strategy.

You don't necessarily have to pay for the top spot in PPC ads: Consider the NFL draft. Teams regularly trade down from their initial spots in the draft because the value isn't there for the player they need in a particular position.

They often can obtain that player even when they pick a little further down in the draft — and ultimately *pay less money* for the player, because the spot where a player is picked goes a long way toward determining his salary.

The same is true of PPC advertising. For some industries, and this includes home improvement, bidding for the top spot costs a lot more than the value it delivers. The top spot for a particular keyword is much more expensive than, let's say, the fourth spot.

Having that top spot makes sense for a business for which people will likely not take the time to perform any additional research — for example, a locksmith or a bail bonds provider. For those types of businesses, people often click on the very first ad that pops up when it's an emergency or time is of the essence.

In that sense, getting a higher position might be worth the investment for your business. If it's critical for your business to be the *very first option* homeowners see when they need help with window coverings, it's worth paying the extra freight for that top spot.

However, when it comes to most home improvement matters, time is not necessarily of the essence. So then there's less benefit to paying for the top spot. An interested party likely will be checking out several providers that pop up for those keywords.

In that situation, ranking third or fourth is just as good as ranking first, and it's substantially less expensive.

PPC also can include display ads: While the focus of this discussion has been PPC ads that appear on search engine results pages, you can also publish display ads on the pages of Google's display ad partners. These are the types of ads you commonly see on larger websites.

In general, advertising for SERPs is intended for to attract customers who are looking to purchase services immediately. Display ads on larger websites are more intended for branding and to attract people who might be interested in your services down the line.

The process for publishing display ads on Google is known as the Google Display Network. Google has "flexible reach" targeting, which ensures greater control over targeting and the ability to try out different targeting combinations more easily.

Remarketing: This also falls under the preplanning umbrella, and it is another great benefit of PPC advertising.

When you do Google Ads, you also can elect remarketing, which means that your ads will continue to make a case for your business with people who have shown an interest in your services by visiting your site previously.

Google can track who has visited your site and continue to display your ads for these leads when they visit other sites. This lets you reengage with leads who did not purchase immediately.

You can even customize the messaging in this ad to make a special offer that will compel them to return to your site and do business with you.

Remarketing has shown to be hugely successful in recent years across a wide variety of industries. It's a marketing strategy that works very well to attract people who are considering improvements to their homes.

An important consideration in remarketing is that you want to set the ads to run only for a particular time frame or to appear only a certain number of times. That way, remarketing targets won't feel like they're being "stalked" by your ads all over the internet. No one wants that, and it would be bad for your firm's reputation.

Thus, remarketing must be employed surgically, and a good marketing firm can help you with figuring out the proper timeframes and/or number of appearances.

Summary of PPC advantages

Virtually instant traffic to your advertisements
- You can have ads on the front pages of Google (and/or Bing and Yahoo) in just few hours.

A world of options print Yellow Pages can't provide
- Use text-based ads, streaming video ads, banner ads, and more.
- Advertise to a targeted audience in minutes.

- Be rewarded for creating good ads with lower ad costs.

Laser targeting
- Advertise to people who are looking *right now* for the services you offer.
- Quickly test to determine which ads bring you qualified traffic.
- Easily monitor which keywords attract visitors who actually convert into customers and which do not, letting you easily alter your ad to include the highest-converting keywords.

Local/regional targeting
- Target users by location, allowing you to specifically reach local customers.
- You can choose where and when you want your ads to be visible.

Cost-effectiveness
- Pay only when a customer clicks on your ad.
- Benefit from free branding even when people don't click on your ad.
- Determine your costs based on your own objectives: Specify exactly how much you want to spend, and even set a maximum daily and/or monthly budget.

Powerful money-making tool
- If you could spend one dollar to make two dollars, how many dollars would you spend?

That's how a well-optimized PPC campaign works.

Measurable results

- You get real-time ROI data through conversion tracking data.
- Every aspect of the process is trackable.
- Google collects and analyzes all key data for you and will auto-send you reports.

Summary of PPC disadvantages

- Only through paying the advertising cost will you be able to determine the ROI of various ads.
- Each new visitor costs money: While you could get some return visitors who bookmark your site, in general when you stop paying, the visitors stop coming.
- Having your ads link to a high-converting site is a must: A good PPC campaign can drive lots of targeted traffic to your site, but if that site doesn't turn visitors into actual customers, it's wasted money.

A note on the landing page

With all that said, a PPC ad campaign is *only as good as the landing page it's selling.*

Let's say you're looking for a home and you drive past a gorgeous billboard advertising an amazing condominium complex just a mile away.

It's advertising resort living at a fraction of the price, tons of amenities, and a great neighborhood. It sounds like paradise

So you head over to the address, full of excitement and glee, and when you arrive, you discover... it's a dump.

It looks like it hasn't been renovated in 100 years, it has a rusty, broken gate out front, and the parking lot is covered in trash that's clearly been piling up for weeks.

Are you going to bother driving onto the property and checking it out? Or are you going to get out of there as fast as you can before you get mugged?

That's what happens when a landing page doesn't deliver what the PPC ad promised.

If the landing page is poorly designed, or if the website isn't selling what the typical visitor would expect, the visitor is going to "click out" in a matter of seconds. And you just paid for a visit that did you no good.

I'll get into landing page and website optimization more in a bit, but it's critical to remember that there's no point to purchasing PPC ads if you're sending visitors somewhere they don't want to be.

Anything from a lack of relevant content to slow page loads can prompt a visitor to set sail in a matter of seconds.

I'll get into website conversions elsewhere in this book, but the bottom line is this: Your PPC ads are only as effective as your website is. Your SEO efforts are only as effective as your website is. Your offline advertising… well, you get the idea.

Just as there would be no point to spending thousands on marketing a pizza parlor with terrible food, health department citations, and a lazy waitstaff, there's no point to driving homeowners to a home improvement business website that has poor navigation, no obvious call to action, and little information on the firm and its services.

The pizza parlor needs to focus *first* on cleaning up the kitchen, improving its food, and hiring better servers. The window treatment site must focus *first* on better serving its visitors and converting them into clientele.

Only then will PPC ads and other marketing methods generate additional revenue.

A site can attract tons of traffic, but if those visitors don't turn into clientele, the traffic is pointless. Once you've transformed your site into a conversion-generating machine, PPC ads will work wonders.

Local Search Optimization

In the most basic sense, when we're talking about local search (you'll sometimes see this capitalized as Local Search, but I'll stay old-school here), we're simply referring to online searches that have a geographical component. (In the window treatment industry, of course, services tend to be extremely localized.)

If you live in St. Petersburg, Florida, and you need to have a replacement odometer installed (by a trained mechanic) for your 2012 Buick LaCrosse, you typically won't simply search for "2012 Buick LaCrosse odometer" or "Buick LaCrosse mechanic" or "2012 Buick LaCrosse repair."

You'll usually add something that *includes your actual location*. So you'll add "St. Petersburg" to your search terms.

(If you're searching in English, you'll far more likely get results for Florida's St. Petersburg than the Russian city, but depending on what the results are, you might need to add Florida.)

Of course, St. Petersburg is also part of the Tampa Bay metropolitan area, with both Tampa and Clearwater each just a short drive away. So you might want to expand your search to Tampa Bay or to each of those particular cities.

But with all of that said... on most devices, the search engine will *already know where you are* and automatically deliver local results, even if you don't add a location. This is usually true as well if you include "near me" in the search.

In recent years, search has become increasingly local. Again, this owes a lot to the massive expansion of affordable mobile technology. Smartphones and tablets (and more recently, even *smartwatches*) let people navigate their neighborhoods easily.

In November 2018, Google noted that *46 percent* of searches have local intent. For a comparison, consider that when I wrote the first edition of this book over six years ago, that number was less than 15 percent. By the time you're reading this, it's likely close to eclipsing 50 percent.

When you limit "local intent" to mobile (specifically smartphone) searches, that number leaps to almost *85 percent* (as of early 2020).

Additionally, according to a fall 2018 survey, 88 percent of searchers who researched a local business on Google continued the process by *calling a local business within 24 hours*.

It's actually rather ironic: In its early days, the internet let us quickly and easily interact with people and places all around the world. These days, we're more likely to use it to find places and services right in our hometowns.

Of course, that's why local search optimization is so critical for window covering businesses in 2020 and beyond. As I noted in the introduction, this is how people will find your business these days.

Some might open up the Yellow Pages if they have that book lying around the house. But many will search on their PC, or tablet, or smartphone.

Optimizing your business for local search ensures not only that you're putting your best foot forward for potential customers — it ensures that you *show up at all*. You need to do this to show up on Google Maps, the most widely used graphical search provider in the world.

Practically every day, I find myself needing to know where something is near my location: an ATM, a gas station, a restaurant, a grocery store.

My phone automatically knows where I am, thanks to GPS. Businesses that are optimized for local search will pop up as soon as I search, and the listings show me how far away they are, directions, etc.

But that's not all: When a business has included its business hours on its **Google My Business** listing, I automatically know whether it's open or closed — or how long I have to get there until it *does* close. (I'll explain GMB more in a bit.)

I can also see ratings and reviews from customers, helping me know whether I can trust that particular mechanic, hair stylist, or retailer.

As I noted before, this is one of the key processes people now use to find local businesses. If you're not taking advantage of it — if your business isn't listed in Google, or if the information there is out of date or incomplete — you're placing yourself at a massive disadvantage compared to your competitors.

Getting to know Google My Business

Let's take a quick look back at the 2013 edition of this book, where I wrote:

Your first thought might well be that Google+ Local is an extraordinarily silly name for what is now one of the most important marketing tools for local businesses.

And you're right.

Google likes silly names for its services. It also likes changing names, so maybe you won't be stuck with it for too long.

Well, what do you know? In 2020, not only is that extraordinarily silly name gone, but it's *long* gone. As in several years gone.

The name itself was part of Google's branding of its social media service, Google+ (aka Google Plus), which failed rather spectacularly itself.

Google does a *lot* of things right, and if I haven't mentioned this enough already, Google is absolutely imperative to the success of every small business, including window treatment businesses.

But one thing Google still hasn't been able to crack is social media. It's taking a somewhat different initiative on that with Google My Business, but we'll talk more about that in the social media chapter.

For now, let's look at how Google My Business — GMB for short, naturally — relates to local search.

It's useful to understand a little history here:

In the mid-2000s, Google had a few different names for its local business listing platforms. It started with Google Local, Google Maps, and the Google Local Business Center.

Over the next few years, well, it got confusing. Google Local and Google Maps merged, with the new combination briefly taking the name Google Local and then switching to Google Maps.

A few years later, the company launched "Google Place Pages for Google Maps." A little later (June 2011), we finally saw the arrival of Google+, which

Google intended to be a true rival to social platforms such as Twitter and Facebook.

In its wake, virtually everything became Google+ branded. We got Google+ Pages, Google+ Your Business, Google+ Brand, Google+ Local...

Anyway, we'll cut to the chase. Google+ (the social platform) was virtually dead on arrival, although Google kept trying to make it a thing for several more years. It finally gave up in 2018. As you read this, Google+ is relegated to the dustbin of history.

Instead, we have **Google My Business**, which is essentially one-stop shopping for everything that used to fall under the umbrella of Google+ Local, Google+ Your Business, Google+ Places, etc.

GMB itself actually has been around several years now, but it's become more firmly entrenched as "*the* Google tool for small business" in recent years as Google has clarified its suite of tools.

A few reasons why I broke down that history for you:

1) You need to remember that as great as Google is at many things, it also initiates a lot of tools that fail and/or end up being reworked or renamed. That's the nature of such a creative industry.

2) The digital marketing landscape changes all the time. To be competitive, you need to stay current — or at least hire a marketing company that stays current *for you* and is constantly evolving along with the changes.

3) Regardless of all the rebranding of Google's tools, it is *completely dedicated* to helping

small businesses market themselves online. And that all starts with Google My Business.

As you already know, yes, many people review window treatment companies and other home improvement services on Yelp and other review sites, such as Google and Facebook's review platforms and on Angie's List. Having the strongest reputation in your area immediately makes you a frontrunner for these services.

Surveys show that 72 percent of consumers consider online reviews as trustworthy as personal recommendations, which is why ensuring you have positive (and preferably exceptionally positive) reviews on your GMB listing is so important.

At Ring Ring Marketing, we utilize a proprietary email program that solicits reviews from homeowners in a thoughtful manner. It's a great way to generate more reviews without running afoul of Google's prohibition on "review gating," a scheme in which customers are essentially only allowed to post positive reviews.

Our system encourages a positive review process without crossing the line into mandating positive reviews. (I discuss review generation in greater detail later in this book.)

Your GMB listing also effectively acts as a blog, thanks to the Google Posts feature. You can provide updates and reach out to customers, providing useful information and showing potential customers you're highly engaged and communicative.

Publishing short updates on Google Posts also helps with your website SEO (because Google sees you more as an influencer in your industry), so you're getting two benefits every time you post!

Don't forget Bing Places for Business

Of course, Bing has its own local option, and while it makes sense to make Google My Business your top priority, that doesn't mean you should entirely ignore Bing.

While Bing comprises a comparatively tiny portion of the search market — speaking of great branding, there's a reason you never hear someone say "just Bing it" instead of "just Google it" — Bing still plays a role.

And that's simply because Bing is Microsoft's search engine, and Microsoft remains an enormous player in computing, thanks to its popular Windows software.

That's why when you buy a new laptop or desktop computer with the Windows operating system, the default search engine (on Microsoft's default web browser, Microsoft Edge) is Bing.

Granted, most people with even a modest understanding of technology know they can change their computer's default web browser in just a couple of minutes. (It's incredibly easy.) So if they prefer a browser such as Google Chrome to Microsoft Edge, as many do, they just make the change.

(Note: As of early 2020, Chrome had 65 percent of the web browser market share, compared to just over 4 percent for Microsoft Edge. Microsoft's previous browser, Internet Explorer, actually had a little over 10 percent of the market share.)

Additionally, virtually all smartphone users in the United States either use Android devices (Android is a Google operating system) or iPhones (Apple). As of this writing, about 42 percent of people used Android phones, while 57 percent used iPhones. The other operating systems *combined* comprised a fraction of 1 percent. So Android and iPhone really are the only contemporary players in the market.

Regardless, there's no reason not to ensure your window treatment company is properly listed on Bing Places for Business (previously known as Bing Local).

Your window covering business has a physical address, so it likely already has a Bing Places for Business listing. You simply have to claim it.

Much like Google My Business, you'll want to ensure your profile is completed with all the pertinent information for your business.

Note that if you haven't filled out your Bing Places for Business listing previously, you might have an even more convenient option. Bing actually lets you *import* the information from your GMB account, if you wish. (This won't affect your GMB listing.) It's right there in the setup process.

Just make sure that you've checked all the information in your Bing listing after the import. Don't just assume it's all correct.

Unlike GMB, Bing Places for Business doesn't have its own native reviews. Instead, it's partnered with Yelp (as with Yahoo, we're going to leave off the exclamation point for simplicity), one of the most popular online review services.

However, other reviews from third-party services can appear on your Bing Places for Business page.

There are some other differences between these two platforms, and it's useful to note that Yahoo has a local platform of its own, but most of the points noted earlier about Google My Business relate to all the services.

The most important takeaway is that completing all your window treatment business's information on these platforms — and ensuring it's accurate and kept up to date — is necessary for putting your best foot forward when people are searching for local businesses. These services are built to accommodate mobile users, a segment that has grown massively in the past few years.

Citations

Another very important aspect of local search optimization is the use of **citations**. These are mentions of your business that appear on the internet *regardless* of whether there's an actual link to your website.

To superpower your local SEO, you must generate a substantial number of local citations.

A local citation could occur when your home improvement business is noted in general text in an online listing of companies in your local market or your region. It could be a mention in a news story, white paper, or trend piece.

Although these references to your business don't include a direct link, they are key components in the ranking algorithms of Google and other top search engines.

The more you're referenced on other sites, especially if they're among the more regularly visited and indexed sites, the more "useful" the search engines think your business is. This improves the rankings of your business's website.

A citation on something such as a chamber of commerce or county business index is especially useful. This is also true of a citation in a major newspaper or other news site.

That's because these citations lend even more legitimacy and credibility to your site — it's awfully hard to "fake" an appearance in a major newspaper, so the search engine knows you're an actual operating business.

Your internet marketing specialist can help you learn how to improve your citations, but in general, the key is to ensure you're properly listed in all legitimate listing services that are appropriate for your business.

Be sure you're included in local blogs, locally focused directories, and directories/blogs that are specific to home improvement.

If you're involved with something newsworthy that can get your business named in a newspaper story or on a local television station's website — such as providing free products and services for a family in need or a cherished member of the community — that's a great citation to have.

Quick tip: Doing community service such as this is a spectacular way to get publicity, because the local news rarely covers such businesses (excepting paid advertising) outside of brief listings, and news stories are the types of citations Google and other search engines will prioritize.

Local search advantages

- It's free, which allows for infinite return on investment.
- It lets customers rate and review your business, so if you're good at what you do, you'll stand out from the crowd.
- It adds your site to Google Maps, one of the top ways people discover local businesses now.
- It lets you add specific keywords to your business description, giving you a leg up on window covering competitors who have not done this.

Local search disadvantages

- Only seven businesses automatically show up as a search result.
- It can take greater than a month to show up in the listings, and the likelihood of appearing high in the results (or in the first seven at all) depends on optimization.
- You can only optimize your business for the five to ten most relevant keywords.

Search Engine Optimization (SEO)

An entire book can be written about search engine optimization (SEO). In fact, many have been, and many more will be. There are many facets to SEO, and the best practices are regularly changing. Frankly, they've changed substantially just in the four years since the previous edition of this book.

Here, I'll touch on the highlights.

You undoubtedly know the purpose of SEO: It's a set of processes intended to help ensure your window covering website/landing page ranks as highly as possible in search results.

Ever since search engines began appearing on the internet, website owners and webmasters have understood the power of ranking as highly as possible on SERPs.

It's not exactly a new concept: Everything else being equal, you're more likely to get people's business if *yours is the first option they see*.

That's why print magazines (yes, a few still exist) want to be at the *front* of the racks in physical bookstores (if you can still find one of those today — it's not easy).

That's why businesses for many years would select names that put them at the front of white pages and Yellow Pages listings:

Ace Plumbing was upstaged by Abacus Plumbing, which was eclipsed by Aardvark Plumbing, then A Aardvark Plumbing, followed by A AA Aardvark Plumbing... I'm sure you remember how that went. You'll still see a lot of local businesses today using this tricky naming process.

Today, however, alphabetization doesn't matter much. Search engines don't care whether your business name starts with an A or Z. They take no notice of whether you have a really colorful name or a bland one — that's not part of the equation.

Granted, your business's name *does* matter, but only in the sense that the SEO will be improved if *terms in the name are highly relevant* to what people will be searching for.

That is, if instead of handling window covering services, you happened to sell custom hubcaps in Charlotte, naming your business Charlotte Custom Hubcaps (and snagging that as a domain name as well) would be a big help for your SEO.

If you're a window covering business in Tucson, obviously, something like "Tucson Window Coverings" makes things easiest for search engines and potential leads.

But before we dig into how SEO works, let's start off by defining a few terms:

White-hat SEO vs. black-hat SEO: I touched on these terms earlier, but here's a little more context.

As soon as webmasters realized that search engines were using certain elements of websites to determine how highly those sites should rank, some started to think of ways to game the system.

When a site is using tricks that are only intended to improve rankings or traffic without providing an equivalent benefit to actual visitors, that's black-hat SEO.

On the other hand, when a site uses techniques that improve rankings and traffic that are integral to providing a benefit for visitors, that's white-hat SEO.

Sneaky sites (and their sneaky webmasters) benefited from black-hat SEO for many years, but those days are largely over now. Search engines (particularly Google) tweaked their algorithms substantially to punish sites that used black-hat tactics and reward ones that followed a white-hat approach.

As I noted earlier, it's ***absolutely not worth it*** to work with a firm that promises big results through black-hat practices, no matter how cheap the price.

The money you save up front by working with these con artists — and that's truly what they are — won't come close to making up for the business you lose when Google banishes your site to page eight of its SERPS.

In extreme cases, Google can even *ban your URL altogether*. And once you're on Google's bad side, you're in serious trouble: Google has a *very* long memory.

Spiders/crawling: With rare exception, search engines don't employ people to actually visit websites and determine whether those sites are relevant and useful (and thus worthy of being ranked highly). Instead, they create software known as **spiders**. These spiders go to websites and then read and index the information there, a process known as **crawling** the site.

They don't just review the content visitors can see, but also information in the coding of the site. The info they collect is then factored into complicated algorithms that determine how highly a site should be ranked for various searches people do online.

Organic search results: Otherwise known as natural search results, these are the basic unpaid search results — as opposed to paid listings, "sponsored" listings, or ads — people get when they search for keywords.

As you've surely noticed, searching for anything on Google these days will result in a page of SERPs that include both organic and paid results, and sometimes it can be tricky to tell the difference.

Ultimately, your window covering website or has two very distinct objectives.

One objective is to put your best foot forward for actual human visitors. You want people who visit your site to be impressed by your business and the specific window treatment products you sell and install.

Your ultimate goal is to create *conversions*, which essentially means that the site prompts the visitor to take an action toward becoming a customer.

For a window treatment business, a conversion most often would be considered filling out a contact form for more information or to make an appointment (thus becoming a qualified lead) or going ahead and calling or emailing you directly.

To this end, you want the content on your site to read well, provide useful information, and sell the visitor on the fact that you're a trustworthy and thoughtful provider of home improvement/decorative services.

Beyond dealing with human visitors, the other objective of your website is to sell the relevance of your site to the search engine spiders.

This is where SEO strategies come into play. By employing these strategies in the site's content, design, and coding, you can persuade these spiders to rank your site highly when people search for keywords that would be naturally associated with window treatment sales and installation.

As you might expect, one of the greatest concerns Google and other search providers have is that sites try to game the system to make the *spiders* happy without making actual human *visitors* happy.

This is why Google, in particular, has started heavily penalizing sites that use this approach. It wants the sites that rank highest to be the most useful for *actual people* who are actively searching for what you provide.

You might wonder why certain sites would game the system with pages that rank highly but provide noth-

ing good for the visitors. People will just click out immediately when they realize there's nothing there for
them, right?

Some site owners/webmasters (outside the window
covering industry) do this because their business model
simply pays them for **hits** — visits to sites, whether or
not the visitors bounce out immediately.

These sites use advertising models where it doesn't
matter at all whether the site itself is useful, just that
they've recorded hits for advertisers to the site.

If a visitor goes on to click on an ad on the site, the
site gets paid even more. Ultimately, these sites are not
really selling anything or providing any service; they exist only to trick people into clicking through to the site.

These are the types of sites Google has penalized
with tweaks to its algorithm. Google literally changes its
search algorithm as many as *500 times* in a given year.
Doing so ensures that people searching Google will find
sites that provide the information and products they
want.

This provides a great opportunity for legitimate
business owners such as you. By combining high-quality content with legitimate white-hat SEO techniques,
you make *both* your human visitors and search engine
spiders happy.

When your written copy is relevant, easy to read,
and compelling — not just stuffed with irrelevant keywords to trick the spiders into ranking you more highly
— you'll actually be increasing your SEO and receiving
higher rankings (and thus increased traffic).

It's a lot harder to game the system now, and that's
not a bad thing at all: It means legitimate websites such

as yours are rising to the top while the tricksters are relegated to the depths of the SERPs.

At the risk of belaboring this point, I need to be clear: Sites that use black-hat tactics are massively penalized when Google figures out what's happening. (And Google *always* finds out.)

They can plummet so deep in search rankings that no one will ever see them, and when the tricks used are particularly egregious, Google (and Bing, Yahoo, etc.) can even remove the site completely from search rankings.

If an internet marketing "expert" claims he or she can substantially improve your site's rankings or traffic without making substantial improvements to the actual content, design, and relevance of the site, don't walk away — *run*.

Trying to trick Google is a very, *very* bad idea. Instead, find a legitimate internet marketing pro with a great white-hat SEO record.

Great original content is great, but sham experts will rip off content from other sites and use it on yours. Relevant incoming and outgoing links are great, but these scammers will add links from hundreds of irrelevant websites.

They'll hook you into massive link exchange sites that provide nothing useful for your actual human visitors. The brief jump your site might see in rankings is not worth the damage that will occur when the hammer comes down.

Doing it the right way

So how do you do it the right way? It's important to understand what a search engine is looking for when determining how highly your window treatment site/landing page should rank in SERPs.

Although this relates to all major search engines, let's just use Google as an example. Every time someone does a search for certain keywords, Google's search engine considers the following:

Site authority: Is your site an authority on what the searcher is looking for? Having lots of high-quality, original content regarding the subject (in your case, information related to window treatments) signals that it is. So do incoming links from other legitimate sites Google considers authoritative on related home improvement and home renovation subjects.

By filling your site with original content that informs and educates people on how they can improve their homes, you're signaling to Google that you're an authority on the industry — while simultaneously establishing *trustworthiness* with human visitors that you'll take good care of them and their most valuable investment.

Social media: I'll discuss social media in much greater detail later in this book, but the more citations your site receives in social media, the more authoritative it appears on the subject.

Site performance: If your site receives lots of visitors, that's a big help. If those visitors not only stick around but also click on several other pages contained in the site, even better. Google tracks all these things, and they all affect your SEO.

You can view this as a cyclical process: The more visitors you get, the better your site will rank. The better your site ranks, the more visitors you get.

So once you get that engine running, it virtually sustains itself. And your window covering business website keeps growing in authority and popularity.

Content: *This doesn't just mean the words on the site.* This also means images, videos, and other media relevant to what the searcher is looking for. The more *original* the content you populate your site with, the better.

I like to say that **content is king**, and for good reason: More than anything these days, the quality of your content will determine how well (or how poorly) your site ranks.

I talk more about content elsewhere in this book, but the key thing to remember is that your site *absolutely needs good content*. There's no shortcut around this that will produce the SEO and conversions you need.

I realize that many window covering businesses don't have the in-house resources to generate lots of strong content themselves. If that's the case for you, you should consider contracting out for content.

You can do so by either contracting directly with a qualified independent freelance writer or working with an experienced marketing company that has a team of solid writers.

The latter option typically works best, because you won't have to worry about all the administrative aspects of working with an individual contractor.

Site design: Sites that are well designed are not only most helpful to human visitors, but to spiders as well.

A well-designed site makes it easy for the spiders to interpret how relevant the site is to what people are looking for. A properly designed site also includes keywords in its image tags and coding to communicate relevance.

As for how to employ all these techniques and practices, that's a subject for a book that's much more specific to SEO.

You can use such resources to learn more about determining what keywords to use in your copy and coding, designing your site for maximum impact on human visitors and spiders, and tracking how well your site is doing compared to your competitors. Regularly analyzing and tweaking your approach is *absolutely necessary*.

If, like most window covering business owners, you prefer to concentrate on running your business, a professional internet marketing professional can handle all those elements for you.

Just remember to find a provider who uses white-hat tactics and can provide great examples of having increased sites' rankings through the legitimate methods detailed here.

It's always most beneficial to work with a company that has experience in window fashions or at least home improvement in general. You don't want to contract with an agency that markets you the same way it markets hair salons or sandwich shops.

Link building

As with SEO in general, link building is a broad subject. It's an essential part of SEO, because search engines still place a lot of importance on which sites your window covering business website links *to* (**outgoing links**) and which sites link to *you* (**incoming links**).

If your website is an island unto itself, that suggests to Google that your site is not very useful or influential, regardless of whether that's true.

That's why so much black-hat SEO is focused on artificially building up rankings based on link networks and purchased links. Not all link networks are necessarily "tricks," and not all purchased links are necessarily irrelevant, but they've been used so irresponsibly that it now requires great care to ensure you don't make Google think you're up to no good.

When you build links appropriately and organically, you're employing a powerful tool for your site. I'll go over a few of the basics here:

In essence, every live webpage in existence has the ability to "vote" for other webpages by linking to them.

How many votes are provided by an incoming link depends on several factors, but a key one is the *SEO strength* of the site that's voting.

How much the votes from that incoming link affect your SEO also can depend on the *relevance of the linking website to yours*.

That's why getting inbound links from influential sites specifically related to home renovation is extremely useful.

It's also important to consider **link velocity**, which refers to how quickly your site acquires new links. If your site gets hundreds or even thousands of new links in one fell swoop, that's far less beneficial than steadily aggregating links over a matter of time.

If your window covering business site suddenly gets lots of new links, that's a *huge red flag* for Google. If it steadily builds links over time, Google interprets that as a natural process for a site that's properly growing in influence.

The best way to get other sites to link to yours is to *create useful, interesting content* about home improvement. A blog that's specific to your main focus is thus incredibly beneficial for attracting links.

Post regularly with original copy that's relevant to sites you want to link to yours. Make sure the copy is clean and grammatically correct: No one wants to link to a site that reads like it was written by Yoda after a three-day bender.

Also, don't only write copy that specifically sounds like you're pitching your window covering business and its services. While it's fine to mention your business on occasion, you're far more likely to attract incoming links if you're providing solid information that's *useful for everyone.*

As I'll discuss further in the social media section, it's smart to blog about matters that are interesting to homeowners in general, even if the subjects aren't specifically about window coverings. Your blog will generate a lot more readership and interest if it covers a broad spectrum of issues.

Also, adding images, infographics and other types of content specific to home renovation makes your blog more SEO-attractive.

Again, you'll probably have to contract out for content generation, unless you have someone on staff who's truly great at writing interesting, SEO-friendly copy (and whose time you can free up to work on it).

Other ways to encourage links:

- **Make it easy for people to bookmark your posts and forward them to friends.** Several tools let people do this with a single click. This is a great way to make posts go "viral" and gain links. (Remember, virtually any time of business — including a window covering business — can create interesting content people will want to share. Open your mind about all the subjects you can cover. Just make sure you don't get into any controversial territory.)

- **Include a link back to your website when you comment on other sites and blogs.** Most sites include a field for that, so use it. Obviously, be sure your comments are interesting and colorful, and that they represent your business in a professional manner. You never want a controversial comment — and *especially not a crude or profane comment* — linked to your business site. If you delegate commenting you a staff member, make sure he or she knows to always communicate in a thoughtful manner.

- **Submit your site to directories.** There are many different directories — some free, some requiring a paid membership — that will be included as incoming links when you get listed with them. Obviously, be sure to list your site with directories that are specific to home improvement/renovation, along with your local chamber of commerce.

- **Link to other relevant sites whenever possible.** This refers to **reciprocal links**, which can be tricky. They aren't nearly as beneficial when they appear to search engines to simply be a one-for-one trade. (It's exactly like "I'll follow you if you follow me back" on Twitter.) However, in general, outgoing links help SEO when you're linking to quality sites, and sometimes those sites will link to you down the line. This will not hurt your SEO. Think of it as karma. Like the Beatles said, "the love you get is equal to the love you give."

How to get in trouble: If you really feel like playing with fire and want to risk upsetting Google (and Bing/Yahoo), the best way is to obtain incoming and outgoing links by buying and selling them.

Search engines — and once again, I'm referring to Google in particular — truly *despise* the selling of links. It sets off all sorts of alarms that something bogus is going on. Buying links, while not quite as dangerous as selling them, also tends to backfire.

Build your links naturally and organically. I'll quote directly from Google's 2020 language about link schemes:

The best way to get other sites to create high-quality, relevant links to yours is to create unique, relevant content that can naturally gain popularity in the Internet community. Creating good content pays off: Links are usually editorial votes given by choice, and the more useful content you have, the greater the chances someone else will find that content valuable to their readers and link to it.

As with SEO in general, there's more to generating great incoming links, but these are the basic tenets to keep in mind.

CHAPTER 2
Mobile Marketing

You'll recall that smartphones and tablets were mentioned something like 1 million times in the fore-word and introduction.

Well, okay, maybe it wasn't quite that much. But I mentioned those technologies a lot, and honestly, there's no way to mention them *too much*. Because much like internet marketing is marketing in this digital age, the mobile internet isn't just the future — it's the present.

As of early 2020, we've reached the point where smartphones are *omnipresent* in the United States and all developed countries.

Today, they're easy to use, affordable, and incredibly convenient. Fifteen years ago, they might have been mostly limited to people in their wage-earning years, but now, teenagers (and even some adolescents) have their own smartphones. Grandparents and even great-grandparents have their own smartphones.

Of course they do. If you have teenagers, you want to know you can contact them anytime they're out of the house—and that they can contact you as needed. If you have parents in their seventies or eighties, you want them to be able to call you as needed for assistance or whatever else they need.

Over the past decade, and especially in the last five years, smartphones have become a staple of everyday life for every generation.

If you were born in 2000, you almost certainly have a smartphone. If you were born in 1980, you almost certainly have one. If you were born in 1960, you almost certainly have one.

Even if you were born in *1950*, recent stats indicate, there's about a 50/50 chance you own, *and regularly use*, a smartphone in 2020.

An early 2018 survey by Pew Research Group found that 95 percent of Americans owned a cellphone of some kind, with 77 percent owning a smartphone. Over 18 months later, it's safe to assume the latter number has eclipsed 80 percent.

The same study showed that 89 percent of Americans ages 30-49 owned a smartphone, followed by 73 percent of those ages 50-64, and 46 percent of those over 65.

Again, as rapidly as smartphone use has grown over the past year, it's safe to assume each of those statistics has risen at least a few percentage points.

If we generalize to just Americans over 55 a more recent study from Deloitte noted that *74 percent* owned smartphones.

That survey further noted that "smartphone growth was *strongest among older age groups* at over 10 percent" and that "Americans are viewing their smartphones more often than ever before, on average *52 times per day*."

All of which makes perfect sense. Think about when you got your first cellphone. Suddenly, your landline didn't make a whole lot of sense anymore. You now had a phone in your hand that you could take anywhere.

What use was it to have a phone that was wired to a wall back at your home?

If you still have a landline in your home (you have one for your window covering business, of course), it likely serves as only as a complement to your mobile phone.

Similarly, the desktop computer is increasingly becoming only a complement to a laptop, smartphone, or tablet. Americans now access the internet *much more often on mobile technologies* as they do from home. And that's especially true of smartphones.

In the 2015 edition of this book, I noted that "people under 30 are used to accessing information on the go. With your type of business, they will not represent a large percentage of your clientele now, but they will increasingly over time."

It's amazing how things change in just four years. We can now substitute "30" for "40" or even "50," and one could argue we're on the verge of going with "60." (Look for that in the next edition!)

Kids today know how to operate an iPhone or Android phone before they even enter grade school. Adults in their thirties and even those pushing 40 have been accustomed to communicating through mobile technology for much of their adult lives.

And it's very important not to dismiss the effect of mobile technology on older generations. A decade ago, you might not have expected people over 60 to be interested in carrying mobile phones. In 2020, many have abandoned their landlines and use their mobile phones exclusively.

Mobile marketing takes many forms, but in essence, it's simply the process of marketing and promoting your business through mobile technologies (particularly smartphones), whether through your website, social media, text messaging, or other means.

This is where your audience exists now. While some still get their online information through desktop computers, mobile use has eclipsed desktop use for good.

Defining a broad term

The concept of mobile marketing preceded the explosion in smartphone and tablet use, but the term had a more limited definition, for the most part, previously.

For example, the first thing many people thought of regarding the term mobile marketing was text messages, more specifically **SMS**, which stands for short message service.

This later expanded to **MMS** (multimedia message service), which let companies text users who opted-in to the service with images, audio, and video. Both technologies remain aspects of many companies' mobile marketing campaigns.

Another aspect was the innovation of **QR codes**, which let a user to scan a 2D image with the phone's camera instead of typing in a URL or doing an online search.

By including these images on posters, signs, magazine advertisements, etc., the company provided a simple way for the user to go straight to a website to access information or buy something.

However, QR codes never really caught on. Few businesses bother using them anymore, and I don't recommend their use for window covering business clients in 2020.

The only codes consumers typically scan these days with smartphones are **UPCs** (universal product codes), which let them easily research products in retail stores. (They also come in handy for scanning food products in apps such as MyFitnessPal, letting users easily determine calorie counts and related metrics.)

Today, mobile marketing has taken on a much broader definition. It now encompasses the type of marketing and promotion you would do for PC users, but for people now accessing the internet on phones.

For example, many websites are built to display well on laptop or desktop computer monitors. You can view them in Google Chrome, Microsoft Edge, or Mozilla Firefox browsers to ensure they display correctly.

Those same sites, however, *display very differently when viewed on a smartphone*. They can be hard to read and hard to navigate on smaller displays.

This has led many businesses to create mobile versions of their sites. The site knows it's being accessed from a mobile phone and defaults to a mobile version.

Other businesses take this process a step further and create Android or iOS apps for their phones, letting the user simply tap an app to access functions of the business.

In 2020, it's *more important that your window covering business website be optimized for mobile users* than for desktop users. That's not just an opinion: It's the way search engines such as Google do business.

In 2018, Google officially implemented its **mobile-first index**. Here's the simplified explanation: When determining how highly to rank your window covering website, Google places much more weight on the mobile **user experience** (abbreviated as UX) than on the desktop experience.

In other words, if your site looks great and works well on a desktop computer but looks bad and is hard to navigate on a smartphone, Google *pushes you down in its rankings*.

If your site works wonderfully on a smartphone but not so well on the desktop, your site will rank better than the other way around.

Of course, I strongly recommend your site be optimized for *both* mobile and desktop users. For an industry that specifically targets homeowners, it's critical to have a great UX for both.

However, if you had no other choice but to choose one UX to optimize, *it must be mobile*. That ensures that best rankings in search results and the best overall experience for homeowners.

Mobile marketing is *the* key tool for local businesses

Mobile marketing is most critical for businesses such as window treatment companies, who do all (or *virtually* all of their business) *locally*. Because you have a brick-and-mortar business that relies on local customers, it's imperative that your marketing efforts not only include mobile, but make it a priority.

As I indicated above, it's time to stop thinking of your website or your online ads as being seen most often on a large monitor attached to a desktop computer.

Please forgive the bold type that follows, but I don't want you to miss this point:

Those days are over. Just like Google, it's time for you to think <u>mobile-first</u>.

Some people will view your site on a desktop, sure, the same way some people were still listening to audio cassettes when the rest of the world was moving to compact discs, or how some still watched VHS tapes after DVDs arrived — and how a few stragglers are still listening to CDs and watching DVDs today, even though most of the world has moved past physical media and on to digital music and video.

Increasingly more people are viewing your site on a smartphone, and that will just keep growing in 2020 and beyond. Mobile SEO and Local SEO are now *virtually synonymous*.

If your window covering company's website isn't designed to automatically convert to a user-friendly mobile version when viewed on a phone, you'll lose virtually every customer who pulls it up on a smartphone.

Not only does it take a lot more effort to read a fully featured site on a small screen, but you'll be seen by the visitor as hopelessly behind the times. If your local competitors have mobile-optimized sites and you don't, you're at a massive disadvantage.

Mobile devices also make it extremely easy to monitor statistics on who's checking out your site and listings, when and where they're viewing it, and which visitors chose to contact you or otherwise convert into a customer. These analytics are critical to optimizing your marketing campaign.

Looking forward in mobile marketing

Consider that virtually everyone is now carrying around a super-powered computer that doubles as a two-way communication device, with GPS and Wi-Fi technology that provides location information on a regular basis.

This is why mobile marketing has overtaken the nature of small business. Billboards simply seek to catch the attention of eyeballs.

Mobile marketing seeks the attention of something that's becoming far more important: a person's personal handheld technological lifeline.

CHAPTER 3
Social Media Marketing

Some people would argue the world was a better place when people could sit down in a restaurant and could resist the urge to look down at their phones every 30 seconds to see whether they had a new notification on Facebook (or Instagram, or LinkedIn, or Snapchat) or a new tweet on Twitter.

Regardless, that's a reality these days. Some people say they're addicted to their phones, and it's hard to disagree. They communicate constantly through social media, and that communication, as noted earlier, increasingly occurs through smartphones.

The giants in social media — Facebook, Twitter, and Instagram (and for younger people, Snapchat) — wield astonishing power to let people and businesses interact with each other in real time. Having a presence on Facebook and Twitter, at the very least, is a requirement for any online business.

Let's look at social media from a return on investment perspective. The biggest benefit to platforms such as Facebook and Twitter is the cost: their basic functions are free.

Sure, there are paid advertising functions that can be used as desired, and you'll see a lot of benefit from "boosting" posts on Facebook, in particular, but it costs nothing to set up a basic Facebook page and start posting.

The same is true of Twitter. They provide a means to reach out to potential clientele at no included cost.

Of course, money isn't the only valuable resource to a business. Time is just as valuable, and the time expended on social media is a factor in its use.

Your business might be set up in a way where you can easily communicate regularly on Facebook or Twitter on a daily basis.

If it isn't — as you'll remember from the content creation directive earlier in this book — you might need to delegate those responsibilities to an employee or contract the process out to a third party, and those options require financial resources.

Whatever the case, every business should have a company page on Facebook at the very least. It's simply expected in today's digital world.

Having a Facebook page — and making sure to post on it regularly, even if it's only a short post or two every day — show that you're active and engaged in today's digital world.

Every time your company adds friends/followers on Facebook or Twitter, you're adding to your firm's branding and influence. Every time you blog about subjects relevant to home improvement and people comment on the posts or link to them, you're expanding your outreach.

However, there's one critical thing to understand whenever you use social media to market your business:

If you use it *unwisely* — being too focused on pitching your window covering company's services or spamming followers with commercial links — you're risking a massive backlash. There are few better ways to sink your social media marketing than by being too commercially oriented.

That might sound strange, given that your whole reason for social marketing is to increase awareness, traffic, clientele, and sales, but it's a quirk of social media.

People don't use social media to be "sold to." They use it to interact and to learn about things of interest to them. There's a lot of room *within that construct* to promote your business, but for the most part, it has to be done ***without a hard sell***.

Use social media to make connections with interested parties. Share information, resources, advice, suggestions. You're a professional in the home renovation industry, so put that knowledge to use.

When people show interest in the services you sell, *that's* the time to provide information along those lines.

Social media can be an incredibly useful resource for business marketing when used wisely, but it can backfire quickly if you let the temptation of the hard sell get in the way.

Build relationships first; sell later.

Is a particular social network worth the time?

Not every social media platform is equal. Facebook and Twitter remain the superstars of the social media world, particularly for homeowners.

Instagram and Snapchat have grown massively in recent years — I hardly mentioned them in the previous edition of this book, to be honest — but their usage remains strongest among younger generations.

With that said, don't sleep on Instagram, because as of early 2020, many younger homeowners (let's say early 30s to mid-30s) have transitioned from Facebook to Instagram.

You're mostly not targeting Generation Z (those born in the mid-1990s to mid-2000s) for window treatments at this time, so there's no powerful reason to concern yourself with Snapchat — at least not yet.

For the biggest bang for your buck, Facebook is still where you want to be. Although it has made some algorithmic changes that massively limit organic reach (which means how many people see your "free" posts), it remains the best platform for targeting your audience.

(With that said, the best social media strategy doesn't *exclusively* target Facebook users. It's never good to put all your eggs in one basket.)

There are only so many hours in the day, and as a small business owner, you need to be able to tell the wheat from the chaff. We've put together a few questions you should consider when determining whether a new social network will drive leads and make your phone ring.

Who is using the network now? Not who the platform wants to use the network. Not who it hopes will use the network. Who is on there *currently*?

You should be able to identify the demographics of the network, how and when its users are interacting with it, why they are using it, and how involved they are.

How likely are these people to use or promote your product? Even if the people using the network fall into your demographic, you need to determine whether they're likely to be interested in the preplanning services you provide.

Are these the type of people using the platform? Is the platform itself set up to easily share items of interest between people using it?

The networks that provide the best return on investment tend to be the ones in which social sharing elements are integral to the platform and consistently used.

Facebook

You know your creation has become a landmark aspect of popular culture when someone makes a major feature film about both your creation and you.

The Social Network might not have always portrayed Facebook inventor Mark Zuckerberg in the kindest light, but the film's very existence showed what a gigantic influence Facebook is in people's everyday lives.

That's true even as newer social media platforms such as Instagram have stolen away some of Facebook's mojo. Younger people, in particular, have fled Facebook in recent years, virtually considering it "their parents' social media."

As quickly as things change, a future edition of this book in five or 10 years might be extolling the virtues of Instagram and barely mentioning Facebook. But that's the future, and in early 2020, Facebook remains a major player.

Even as younger people have moved on from Facebook, the platform has *continued to grow in use overall*. That's right. As we close in on 2020, Facebook is far from dying. It's still growing.

Granted, the growth is slower these days than it used to be. In fall 2018, it reported "only" adding 22 million new daily users worldwide. That's small for Facebook, but hey, it's still 22 million more people.

In the last edition of this book, I noted that Facebook had "an astonishing 800 million active users as of this writing."

You know what's really astonishing? In just four years, Facebook is now up to *2.3 billion users*. It's virtually tripled that once "astonishing" number since 2015.

Facebook has become a constant companion in people's lives. And again, it's important to remember that Facebook is the more convenient, even the most *comfortable*, platform for middle-aged and older people.

It's incredibly convenient and easy to use. Mothers and grandmothers love it for keeping up with their families and distant friends. They're not giving it up anytime soon.

Advertising on Facebook: The social engagement aspect of Facebook is obviously useful, but again, it has its limitations, such as the need to avoid a hard-sell approach.

Facebook paid advertising is an entirely different animal. The platform provides tools that let you place ads that will conform to people's interests across Facebook.

This isn't a good place to get into the specifics, for two reasons. First, it can be a bit complicated. Second, Facebook revises its advertising approach constantly, so best practices today could be very different by next week.

Whether Facebook advertising will provide a good return on your investment is something to consider thoughtfully, preferably with the assistance of an internet marketing professional. I can tell you that many clients have seen excellent ROI on thoughtfully crafted Facebook advertising campaigns.

Boosted posts on Facebook

For any type of business, having some sort of presence on Facebook is a must. It's a largely simple and completely free way to build your brand, market your services, and communicate to your customers.

Actually, let's get back to that "completely free" thing for the moment. Yes, it's still technically free, but as with any very successful social media platform, Facebook is looking to monetize its services.

If you use Facebook, you've probably noticed the ability to "boost" your posts, which costs money.

Boosting your posts lets you increase the time your post is seen by your friends, in addition to increasing the likelihood the post will be seen.

These days, Facebook really wants business to pay at least something for the promotion they get through the service. To that end, it changed its algorithm to massively depress the "organic reach" of posts on Facebook business pages.

In other words, the vast majority of unpaid posts you publish will not be seen in your followers' news feeds. It's unfortunate, but that's the deal. Recent studies show that organic reach today could be as low as *2 percent*.

For this reason, it's smart to ***boost selected posts***, particularly ones where you're pushing a big sale or new service. Followers will see your window covering company as an expert in this area and likely turn to you for these services.

Facebook Search: What you need to know

Facebook's search function pulls up relevant information based on you (the searcher) — your interests, your pastimes, what you care about.

In other words, your search results will be different from those of other searchers, because Facebook already knows what you're interested in, based on your Facebook activity and connections.

Facebook hopes that instead of simply using Google Search to find businesses and people of interest to you, you'll use its internal search function, which it believes will get you what you're looking for faster and more efficiently.

What this means to your window covering business is that you should ensure you're active and well represented on Facebook, both on your own page and in interacting with users. That will increase the likelihood that people using Facebook Search will find your business.

Not only that, but you'll be prequalified by "Likes" from those users' friends and people within their fields of interest.

What's cool about Facebook Search is how it weights aspects that are similar to those of people (or businesses) to which you're connected on Facebook. For example, places that your connections "Like" or perform a check-in will show up higher on your search.

Facebook's search function makes the platform much more useful for marketing purposes, but as a Facebook user, you should also be aware that it makes information you might have considered private — or at least information you didn't necessarily want to broadcast to the world — far more easily accessible.

If you've "Liked" certain pages without much consideration, be advised that Facebook Search can show all that info *unless you've specifically restricted that information* in your privacy settings.

Similarly, if other people have restricted that information in their own settings, you won't get "hits" for them when you perform a search.

As you're likely aware, there's been a lot in the news the past couple of years about Facebook and privacy, in particular the ways it's been monetizing people's data, not to mention concerns about allowing fake news and foreign trolls to shape public opinion.

If you're concerned about that, you're perfectly right to be. If you're especially worried about your personal data (on your personal Facebook page), you should use Facebook's privacy settings to limit the personal information you share.

You can even quit the platform altogether (again, as an individual) if you're truly apprehensive. I get it.

However, this book is about growing your window covering business and how Facebook is a powerful tool for doing that. So if you have concerns about Facebook in general, I suggest weighing those against the great benefits it can provide for your company.

To that end, you should use the Facebook Search function to make sure everything you want users to find when they search for local home renovation services will show up. That means getting your business's social profile in order.

Why? Because these social connections are pretty much the "links" that Facebook uses to determine relevancy and authority.

It's these photos, likes, check-ins, recommendations, etc. that the Facebook Search algorithm will use to qualify and personalize results for Facebook users.

In a very real sense, "Likes" are becoming the "links" of the new digital era on Facebook. What you Like defines you (and/or your business). The more you Like posts and pages related to window coverings (or home improvement in general), the better you'll do in Facebook Search.

Twitter

When Twitter arrived on the scene, business owners were skeptical about how useful this tool could be. If all you can do is post something in 140 characters, how useful can that be?

In fact, it turned out to be extremely useful, especially once it added options to let you write longer posts (with the remainder represented by a link), to include link shorteners (so your characters weren't all used up by a huge link) promoted accounts and posts, etc.

And in 2018, Twitter finally expanded the character count on basic tweets themselves, letting users post up to 280 characters. For reference, the very paragraph you're reading right now (including spaces) is 246 characters. That's plenty of room!

At its heart, Twitter provides a great opportunity to communicate with customers in real time. Because most people use Twitter on their phones, you can connect with followers when they're out and about. And I probably don't need to remind you (again) that virtually everyone is on a smartphone these days.

Because the people who see your tweets are those who already follow you (or have retweeted your tweets to *their* followers), you have a largely *prequalified audience* for your tweets.

And, of course, just like Facebook, it's totally free to tweet anytime you like. (Twitter's promoted posts, just like Facebook's boosted posts, cost money.)

Advertising options for Twitter include **promoted tweets**, which let you promote your window covering business by targeting users who are similar to your current followers and those who have searched terms related to your types of services.

Promoted accounts appear in the "who to follow" section and in search results, appearing on the pages of users that would likely be interested in your brand.

There are other options as well, but what's right for you will depend on what you're looking to achieve.

Even if you don't use Twitter's paid options, it's an amazing way not only to communicate with homeowners in your area, but also to receive immediate feedback. People who won't take the time to send an email are happy to fire off a quick tweet to let you know their feelings about your products and services.

Also, satisfied customers can provide great word of mouth in seconds by tweeting to their friends whenever they have a great experience.

If someone does have a bad experience and posts about it on Twitter, at least you'll know about it right away and have an opportunity to make it right.

Yelp

Yelp was one of the first platforms to mix user reviews with a social media aspect, and it remains one of the biggest.

Although its usage actually dipped slightly in the last quarter of 2018 (for the first time in existence), Yelp still averages more than 178 million unique visitors every month. (By comparison, in the previous edition of this book, that number was 70 million.)

Throughout Yelp's existence, it's at times been an enormous benefit to local businesses — and also a huge pain in the butt. Most businesses have experienced both sides of the coin.

The concept is simple: After people go to local businesses — a doughnut shop, a motorcycle repair shop, a fine restaurant — they post a review on Yelp. These reviews help other people decide whether to frequent the establishment.

If every single Yelp user took care to provide a fair, unbiased, thoughtful review of the particular business, everything would be hunky-dory. You could read through the reviews and determine which ones you felt were most accurate and legitimate.

However, like everything else on the internet, people will try to game the system. Some people try to get perks from the establishments in exchange for a positive review. Some business owners try to run down their competitors with unfairly critical reviews, simply making up facts as they go.

And some people, even if they're not trying to game the system *per se*, just don't take the time to be very thoughtful when reviewing an establishment. If they just happened to be having a bad day, they might rip apart a place (figuratively) even if everything actually was satisfactory.

Yelp has taken steps to deal with all of these issues, and how effective those steps have been might depend on your perspective. The company has created systems to help weed out bogus reviews and keep them from being posted.

If Yelp isn't sure that a review is legitimate, the review gets trapped in the "Yelp filter." A user can only see these "not recommended" reviews by clicking on a specific link. (A big frustration for businesses, of course, is that sometimes legitimate five-star reviews gets trapped in the filter, like a dolphin in a tuna net.)

As for bogus reviews, they're not necessarily always negative: Business owners have been known to sign up under several different accounts and review their own establishments — providing glowing reviews across the board, of course.

The ascendancy of smartphones — you knew they were going to come up again — has only made Yelp more powerful.

Its local search capabilities make it easy to find places near where you are at a given moment and see reviews for those places. You can see why the veracity of those reviews is so incredibly important to business owners.

With all the concern about the veracity of Yelp pages, is it worth it to even participate in the process?

The answer is yes.

Online reviews are not going away, and neither is Yelp. You can't keep people from reviewing your window covering business, like it or not — so you might as well play along. By getting involved, you can help ensure you're being seen in the best light.

As you well know, homeowners don't often contract with a window covering business on a whim. They want to have plenty of information first.

It goes without saying that having several excellent reviews on one of the internet's top review sites provides you a *gigantic* advantage over local competitors who have negative reviews or simply too few reviews.

That's why you can't afford to ignore your reputation on Yelp (or other major review sites).

I should note one more very important fact:

Yelp no longer lets businesses directly solicit reviews from clients and customers, unlike some other review platforms (including Google), so you must be careful not to overtly ask customers to review you on Yelp.

I'll talk about Yelp more in this book's chapter on reviews and reputation, so for more information, head over there.

Blogging

The benefits of having a business blog are almost too great to mention.

Blogging about home improvement in a way that displays expertise provides you enormous credibility, which goes a long way. It lets you communicate about what's going on with your window treatment business. It provides people the opportunity to provide feedback and ask questions through comments.

(And you can moderate those comments before they're posted, removing the risk of spam or other problems.)

Then there's the SEO consideration: When you're generating a lot of content for your website that's at least somewhat relevant to window treatments, your SEO increases *massively*.

Having a strong, regularly updated blog is one of the very best things you can do to increase your website's traffic and search engine rankings.

Blogging also helps you create incoming and outgoing links, which are great for SEO. You can (and should) link to other relevant sites and articles in your blog posts. When you post something of interest to others, it's likely your post will be linked to (or shared through other platforms), increasing your incoming links and traffic to your site.

With all that said, there are some obvious potential downsides to blogging. Spelling, grammar, or fact errors in your posts can make you look unprofessional, so if you're not a good writer (or sufficiently detail-oriented), you should have a better-suited employee or a contracted professional do your blogging for you.

Alternately, you might be a great writer, but you just don't have time to blog. That's another reason to consider delegating the posting process. Whatever the case, the benefit to blogging is almost always worth finding a way to make it work.

Another concern relates to content. Many websites have gotten in trouble (appropriately) with Google for simply duplicating content from other sites in their blog posts.

Not only is this unethical (and in certain circumstances, illegal), but it's a great way to prompt Google, Yahoo, or Bing to drop your search engine ranking into the sewer.

Let's take a second to underline that point: ***Don't copy content from other sites.*** You also shouldn't buy content that clearly wasn't originally written for your site.

Even if you change around a few words here or there or "spin" the copy (a computerized process that rewords sentences), Google has ways of finding it out.

Write original content whenever possible. Posts don't necessarily have to be long; even a couple of paragraphs can be enough, as long as the content is focused on something that interests the homeowner demographic. At RRM, we create original content for window covering business clients that covers a lot of different topics of interest to homeowners. It's really not too difficult.

If you *do* want to share information from another site, no problem: Simply write a sentence or two in a post and link to the site where the article or post appears. You can even excerpt a small amount of the other post, but the key word in that sentence is *small*; too much will get you in trouble.

And whenever you use someone else's content in an excerpt, be certain to include attribution and a link.

As with everything else, blogging is more beneficial for certain types of businesses and services than others, but it has some benefits no matter what you do. Just its ability to improve your site's SEO alone is a good reason to try it.

If this sounds like too great a time investment, speak with a marketing consultant about possible options to outsource the process.

A lot of people make their livings blogging for a variety of different sites, and depending on your needs, these services can be very affordable, especially given the return on investment.

LinkedIn

A social network specifically for business professionals: a simple enough concept, and one that's worked out for LinkedIn to the tune of more than *500 million* members. (That's about *five times* what it had when I wrote the previous edition of this book in 2013.)

Don't get too hung up the term "business professionals." You don't need to wear a suit and tie to work to benefit from LinkedIn. That's how pervasive it has become for business networking.

LinkedIn simply makes it incredibly easy to allow registered users to maintain a list of contact details for people with whom they have some level of relationship. These people are called **connections**.

Once you've made connections, you can connect with people connected to them, allowing you to easily expand your networking base with people in your industry or with common interests/work histories.

You can create a comprehensive profile with a full resume and qualifications, and when you're looking for a new employee or business partner, you can search through LinkedIn users for the experience, skills, and qualifications you're looking for.

LinkedIn also lets you endorse people you've worked with — and be endorsed by the same — with the click of a button. Having your business and various skills endorsed by well-connected users is obviously a great way to gain new business and new opportunities.

Here's the usual caveat: LinkedIn is most beneficial for businesses in which professional networking is an integral part of doing business. However, the platform has a lot of additional tools that can be useful for virtually every type of business owner.

LinkedIn doesn't require constant participation, although the more you participate on the platform, the more helpful it can be.

At the very least, having a LinkedIn profile for yourself is a great way to put your best foot forward and display your skills and abilities to people who might not otherwise know about them.

For a window covering business, linking to other providers in the industry and those who provide related services (albeit not necessarily your competitors) can provide a great foundation for organically building incoming links.

When their sites link to yours, it improves your traffic and your organic SEO, because Google values incoming links from companies in your field very highly.

Google My Business

Your Google My Business page is your virtual business identity in the Google universe. To be able to interact in the Google Plus social network and have followers share your business, you need to have your Google My Business identity set up and ready to share.

GMB has certain social media aspects, including the ability to include your own Google Posts in the platform — something I strongly encourage you to do. It's excellent for engaging with your audience and helps your overall branding and website SEO as well.

I cover GMB rather extensively elsewhere in the book, so I won't go on too long here about its social media aspects.

You're already well aware that Google+ has faded from existence, and as of this writing (early 2020), there was no clear indication that Google would soon take another crack at creating a full-fledged social media platform that could rival the top dogs.

Google Hangouts, which provided users with chat platforms including video chat functionality, similarly failed to catch fire with personal users.

In December 2018, a Google spokesman said the company would be transitioning the classic Hangouts into two other apps, Hangouts Chat and Hangouts Meet, that it currently provides "G Suite" users. (**G Suite** is the term for its brand of business tools.)

The spokesman said both Chat and Meet "will be made available for consumer users, too" but the company has "not announced an official timeline for transitioning users from classic Hangouts to Chat and Meet."

The social media cycle

Ultimately, I hope you choose to include social media in your marketing plan, as it's rapidly becoming expected for all small businesses, including window covering businesses.

If you do so, understand that investing in social media isn't as simple as publishing a couple of posts (or tweets) every day. In fact, there are four key aspects to what's known as **the social media cycle**.

To get the most from social media, you have to eventually participate in all four aspects. Posting is only an element of one of these.

The four quadrants of the social media cycle are:

Social listening: monitoring and responding to customer service and reputation management issues

Social influencing: establishing authority, most often through the distribution and sharing of useful content

Social networking: associating with authoritative individuals and brands, effectively creating a "rising tide that lifts all boats"

Social selling: generating leads and (ultimately) sales from prospects

I'm sure you've noticed that "selling" is the last one on the list, and that might seem strange. You might be

wondering why you would invest time and related resources in social media if the goal isn't to drive business
through sales.

The short version is that *social media isn't really an
immediate sales generator*, at least not for most businesses.

When you dive into social media, don't presume
you'll suddenly see a rapid influx of calls. This is a big-
picture strategy. It's business development for the long
haul.

And that's also why social selling comes *last* in the
process. As I said, people don't want to be hit with a
hard sell on social media.

The successful strategy is to gain their interest, *then*
gain their trust, then weave in occasional pitches for
your services. The "sales" posts must be a small percentage of your overall messaging. Otherwise, you lose trust
your followers' trust — and then *you lose the followers*.

Let's go over each one of the four aspects:

Social listening: This is where you're listening and
responding to your followers' comments on your social
media platforms.

You might get positive comments from homeowners
you served or questions about your pricing or services.
You might get inquiries about special services. You
might be asked how you accommodate certain deed re-
strictions or aesthetic concerns in a community.

What's important is that you're regularly checking
your social media accounts for these comments and responding to them *quickly*. You never want a comment

to go 24 hours without some sort of response, even if it's only a thank you! If you can reply even sooner — within 12 or even 8 hours — that's even better.

Much like responding to reviews (which I'll get into later), responding to social media comments makes it clear that you're focused on customer service.

Remember that you're not just responding to the original commenter. Your response will be viewed by all of your followers. This is an opportunity to brand yourself as a home renovation provider who's responsive and engaged.

Social influencing: This is the "posting" part of the process. It's where you're sharing content that's useful to homeowner demographics and others who are interested in the services you provide.

You might be wondering why people will necessarily follow a window treatment business on social media if they're not actively searching for renovations at that particular time. And that's a fair question.

However, if you're providing content that's useful to homeowners in general, you *will* see your following grow over time.

And as that following grows, you *will* be able to weave in the "social selling" aspect, marketing home improvement services to your followers. They'll be primed to use your window covering company when they're ready to buy.

Social networking: This is an often-overlooked part of the process. It simply means that you want to create connections with other businesses and associations related to home improvement and similar topics.

Of course, I'm not suggesting you network with direct competitors in your area. However, you can follow major associations, and hopefully they'll follow back. You can comment on *their* social media platforms, helping promote your brand and increasing the likelihood you'll get a follow from them. You can also create connections with businesses in your area you partner with or are affiliated with your line of work.

And of course, if you partner with certain noncompeting businesses, be sure to network with them as well.

Share these partners' posts when appropriate. The increases the likelihood that they'll share your posts. It's a lot like having internal and external links on your website. The more connections you have, the more you're seen as your community's local expert. It's a fabulous way to build your brand.

Social selling: Yes, this is the ultimate goal. You'll see benefits (especially in branding) from the other aspects, but at the end of the day, you really want to be selling your services through your social media.

And that's fine. Just keep in mind that if you sell to your followers *too soon* or *too often*, your follower list will dry up faster than a puddle in Arizona in August.

Patience is a virtue here. Try not to do *any* selling for the first few months of your social media plan. You're creating a foundation of trust you can build on later.

When you do include sales-oriented posts, keep them nuanced and light, at least at first. Just pepper them in now and then. No one will be put off by the occasional sales pitch; everyone knows you're a business, after all. You just never want it to be more than 10 percent (or preferably, only 5 percent) of your total posts.

Remember, you want your social media to enhance your online reputation. You want it to show you as an authority on adding value, convenience, and beauty to homes in the area. You want to be seen as a business that reaches out thoughtfully and professionally when any-one notes a concern or has a question on a social media platform.

That's your ultimate goal. When you do all these things, you're viewed as the important community re-source you are, not simply a business.

That all sounds like a lot, I know. I'm not here to tell you that a full-fledged social media plan is an easy thing to implement on your own, because it's not.

Realistically, you'll either need to hire someone who's pretty good at social media to implement this for you or contract out to a reputable marketing company. That's the most efficient and cost-effective way to en-sure it's done right.

I'd just caution you to carefully scrutinize any agen-cies that make big promises of rapid profits from social media. It doesn't work that way. Much like SEO, this is something you need to build up over time — but it will provide substantial results if you stick with it.

Section 2:

Conversions

CHAPTER 4
Maximizing Website Conversions

In the previous edition of this book, I made a point of saying that "internet marketing *is* marketing" now that we're in the digital age.

As you'll remember from the start of *this* edition, I noted that you should feel comfortable with both online *and* offline forms of marketing, as long as you're getting good ROI from both.

It realize it sounds like I'm backtracking on the "online marketing is marketing" idea, but I'm really not.

That is how you have to think of marketing as we turn the corner into 2020 and move forward. As quickly as Americans are adopting digital technologies, you simply can't afford to ignore the internet. It *must* be your top priority.

I just want you to understand that placing the vast majority of your focus on digital marketing doesn't mean you're not "allowed" to keep a toe in the offline pool. That's all.

So with that (hopefully) clarified, let's proceed to the next point:

In the digital age, just as internet marketing essentially *is* marketing, your window treatment business website *is* your business's home.

You might think your business's home is its actual physical structure. As a window covering business, you obviously have a brick-and-mortar location.

Regardless, you need a business address in the *cloud*, which is another way of saying you need a website. You need actual official space on the internet.

It's as crucial as having an office. Your window covering company could change its physical location, but its website is a constant, the place where anyone can find you in this digital age.

In the digital age, where you and your business are physically only matters so much. Where you exist *online* matters a great deal.

Perhaps you're thinking: So what? *Of course* my window treatment business has a website. I pay a few dollars every year or two to the domain provider and hosting company.

My phone number is on there, along with a picture of the business, maybe even a couple of paragraphs about what we do. We display the product lines we sell. We have a few testimonials. I've done my due diligence.

Well, that's just the bare minimum. That's like putting on shoes because the grocery store won't serve you otherwise.

Simply having a website is like simply having a business. It exists. Now what are you going to *do* with it?

Like every other aspect of your business, your website has a purpose. It all ultimately comes down to one thing: *conversions*.

I touched on conversions earlier, but let's dig in a little deeper:

People define "conversions" many different ways. For businesses where the goal is online sales, a conversion is a very simple thing: a sale. It's *converted* a visitor into a paying customer.

There are many analytical methods to determine how effective your website is at attracting new visitors and determining how they got there, how long they spend on the site, what pages they click on, and how long they spend on those pages.

These tools let you see which images, videos, and links they click on. And they let you know what's working — and what's not working — in appealing to new clientele.

I've said it before, and I'll say it again: People are now finding services (and products) online far more than ever before. If they want to find a dog walker, a bike shop, or a psychic, they're finding them *online*.

Businesses that have no website at all? They're in massive trouble. To the ever-growing digital population, those businesses don't exist.

Businesses that have a bare-bones website? They're almost as invisible as those with *no* website. With little-to-no content, no SEO to attract visitors, no incoming links to provide inroads for potential customers, a website like that is a needle in the proverbial haystack.

Businesses with a middle-of-the-road website? That's 100 times better, no question about it. If it has some content, some degree of SEO, and uses some links — and if that's tied in with a touch of social media — that website is actually achieving the minimum standard of what's needed to be successful moving into 2020 beyond.

However, you can do better. The jump from a bare-bones website to a middle-of-the-road one is huge, no doubt. It's like going from a Burger King to an Outback Steakhouse.

It's the next step that makes all the difference, the one that jumps from a chain steakhouse — a perfectly serviceable chain steakhouse, but a chain steakhouse all the same — to a five-star restaurant.

That's the step to a website that's actually oriented toward *converting visitors into customers*. For your industry, it's a website that's designed, built, and maintained with the explicit goal of making your phone ring off the hook with new customers.

This is one of the most powerful revenue generators in modern business.

And obtaining this goal is a lot easier than opening a five-star restaurant. (There's certainly no need to hire a fancy executive chef.) By employing a set of very basic tools, you can turn your website into this powerful revenue generator.

If you're going to have a website — and again, you *need* a website — you might as well put it to work for you. That's what it's there for. If you're not maximizing its potential, you're leaving an incredible amount of money on the table. Don't let that happen.

Designing your website for conversions

Here's the first thing to understand: No visitor will convert to a client until your site has proven itself. Every element of the site must underline your professionalism and credibility — even for a window treatment business.

It must say to the visitor: *We're the right choice for you. There's no need to shop around; we are the solution to your problem.*

That's why someone's visiting your site, right? Someone needs to solve a problem.

If you can convince the visitor that you're the best choice right then and there, you've removed any need for the visitor to leave and keep checking around. *The visitor wants you to be the solution.* You just have to make it happen.

Only after you have proven yourself to your visitors can you focus on converting visitors to paying customers.

Use great testimonials: You have many satisfied customers, right? Ask a few to write a testimonial.

Visitors want to know that real people have been incredibly impressed by the professionalism and care you showed when they've dealt with your business.

You can include more testimonials elsewhere — devote an entire page to them if you like — but use the best ones on all pages where you're trying to compel the visitor to contact you regarding services.

Of course, testimonials are effectively the same as online reviews. I'll get into reviews and reputation later, but you should know that the more great reviews you receive, the better you'll convert website visitors.

Address your visitors personally: The personal touch is very important. People want to know you're a real person who is proud of your business.

Put together some copy — or hire someone with writing experience, if need be — to tell your visitors who you are, how important your profession is to you, and why you're the best person to help them.

Never forget that *your goal is not to sell someone on something.* It's to *help* the person in need, to resolve whatever issue that person has at this time. (They might sound similar, but there's a key difference: Put yourself in the visitor's shoes.)

Show why the visitor should work with you: Here's where you explain why your business is the best option.

Maybe your services are decidedly better than those of the competition. Maybe your prices are better. Maybe it's your experience in the industry.

Think about why someone should do business with you over anyone else. It's like writing a resume or a cover letter when you want a job: The employer has a problem (a job opening) that needs filled, so you're explaining why you're the best person to solve that problem.

Just as in a resume, don't get too bogged down in details: Focus on the most important facts that sell your window covering business on the visitor. Whenever possible, include as many *quantifiable* facts as you can.

This can be a hard nut to crack, but it's absolutely worth the time. Brainstorm with your staff and really figure out why you're the best option for helping your community in times of need. What sets you apart? What is your **unique selling proposition** (USP)?

Once you know this, you can drive that point home on your window covering business website. Know your USP and really impress upon the visitor. That's one of the best ways to drive conversions.

And here's another one:

Call to action: There are some other copy elements that can help reinforce your pitch, but they can vary depending on a number of factors, so let's cut to this integral aspect:

Your site needs a very clear **call to action** (CTA).

Most often for a window covering business, that call to action will be soliciting the visitor to call your telephone number. If the visitor does so through a click on your website, it will be convenient *and* trackable.

The CTA could be to click on your email address link (it *must* be clickable — *always* make it easy for the visitor), which is another thing you can track. It also could be to fill out an information form. (Keep this form short and sweet; that's what you'd want when you visit a site.)

Impress upon the visitor that you're the best option for them, and the solution is just a phone call (or email) away.

Improving your calls to action

The CTA is one of the most important aspects of your website or landing page. You attracted a visitor to your site for one reason: to act in some way.

Everything on your site must be oriented toward converting that visitor, which in your case will either be gathering information on a potential lead or simply making your phone ring. Here are a few ways to improve your calls to action:

Include the CTA on every page on your site: You never want people to have to search for your phone number or email address. Make it easy. If your website it designed so that the CTA is a stable element throughout the site, the visitor can interact with it at any point, on any page.

Specifically, this means you want your web designer to create a **fixed header** (aka a **sticky header**) that stays put throughout the navigation experience. If the user scrolls down on a particular page, this header remains in place. If the user navigates to another page, the header remains.

In addition to ensuring the CTA is clearly displayed throughout your window covering site, this creates a uniform look and feel. No matter where the visitor travels, your business name and contact information is boldly displayed at the top.

Make sure your CTA stands out: You don't want anything on your site to be loud or obnoxious, but make sure your CTA stands apart. Whatever your CTA is, make sure it really "pops" out.

For text CTAs, use a different color for hyperlinks so it's clear to readers that the text is clickable and an action can be taken. For visual CTAs, use a color that starkly contrasts with the rest of your page.

Use strong, active language: This isn't the place to be passive or longwinded. Everything is funneling toward the visitor taking action, so make the CTA clear, simple, and direct.

The visitor should understand exactly what he or she is getting and why acting on the CTA (whether filling out a contact form or calling/emailing you) is the logical thing to do. If that isn't being clearly conveyed, make a change.

Be sure the value of acting is obvious: If you can't explain to a visitor why your offer is going to help in some way, why would the person click through? Your visitor came to the site to gather information about window treatment products and services: The CTA needs to be the solution.

A brief overview of contact fields for landing pages and lead/customer generation

How effective your lead generation is actually can depend heavily on how this form is designed.

According to recent surveys, most marketers consider the lead capture form to have a very significant impact on website performance.

You have a very short window of time to capture anyone's attention when that person visits your page — many experts put this window at a mere *six seconds*.

This rule is something to consider when designing your lead generation form. If the form seems too arduous or time-consuming to fill out, most visitors won't even bother.

The key is finding a balance between getting the information you need and keeping the form simple enough that it won't scare off your visitor.

Some studies indicate that indicated that the optimal number of fields to include is seven, but I don't agree. Keep it simpler than that. Get a name, phone number, and email address. You can also include a field for the visitor to explain what they need.

If you really want to ask for a physical address, I understand, but including that field *could* scare off the lead.

I prefer the strategy of getting basic info at first, "warming up" the lead through marketing emails and related techniques, and then working to obtain a physical address.

If you include too many fields, you'll see a significant drop-off in conversions. If you include too few, you're in danger of missing out on valuable information you might need.

Whatever you do, don't get into the double digits: That's as good as telling visitors you don't consider their time valuable. They're providing you information, not taking the SAT.

Contact Us

First Name *

Last Name

Phone *

Email *

Consultation Needs:

Security Code *

wdws9

Submit

Keep in mind that there's a big difference between what information you'd *like* to have and what you *need* to have.

Name, email address, and phone number are essentials, obviously. For your type of business, you *might* ask for a ZIP code and/or and some other demographic information, such as household income or age range.

But again, the more fields you include, the fewer conversions you're likely to get.

Ultimately, one of the best things you can do is review your landing page as if you were simply a visitor: Would you want to fill out that form? What advantage will you get from providing your contact info?

If your responses aren't overwhelmingly positive, you'll want to make some changes.

Grabbing your website visitor's attention right from the top

Visitors are great, right? Well, maybe not visitors to your home, at least when they're annoying in-laws or someone selling appliances door to door. But getting visitors to your business website is great.

If they're coming to your site, you're popular. You can check the analytics and see where they're coming from and what brought them there.

Of course… visiting the site is only half of the process, and you don't get any credit for half. A half-baked cake isn't something you want to eat. A half-vacuumed carpet just looks worse than a carpet that hasn't been vacuumed at all. You know what they say: Close only counts in horseshoes.

As I noted previously (yes, I repeat myself when something is *really* important), visitors do you no good if you can't convert them into customers.

It's like having the most-visited art gallery in town, but if no one ever buys a painting, you'll be the most popular artist begging for quarters on the street.

Your site can't just be focused on attracting visitors — it needs to *actively sell* those visitors on what you can exclusively provide them. It needs to get the point across right away.

How do you do that on your site? For one thing, figure out your top selling point to customers and try to make that the first thing they see.

Your business's name is all well and good, but that alone doesn't sell the customer (unless your business is named Bill Gates' Free Money for Everybody Inc.).

Use that valuable real estate at the top of your site to sell your visitors on what your window covering business does better than anyone else: your *USP.*

Whatever you do best, whatever your claim to fame, spell it out clearly and make sure visitors can't miss it. If that's the best price, the best services, whatever it is, *don't be shy about it.*

A note about SEO: As I noted earlier in this book, an integral aspect of ranking highly in search engine results is incorporating relevant keywords in your copy.

These need to be in there, but far too many sites use keywords incorrectly. They stuff copy full of keywords to the point where the writing sounds like it's intended for the spiders (the search engine software that crawls the site), not for the visitor.

Never do this.

It will send visitors racing for the "exit." It looks especially amateurish on a window covering business website, but it honestly looks bad no matter what business you're in.

A qualified internet marketing expert can help you learn how to incorporate keywords so they sound natural in the copy.

Also, when keywords are used *too* often, this can actually *hurt* your SEO. Counterintuitive as it might seem, clunkily jamming in "window coverings" or "new blinds" into every single paragraph works *against* you.

The search engines will penalize your site in the rankings if the keywords appear too often, or not in the right places.

Yes, it's important to serve two masters, the human visitor and the search engine spiders, but always err on the side of writing intelligent, compelling copy for the visitor.

Nothing will undermine your credibility faster than copy that makes little-to-no sense because it's only there to drive search engine rankings.

Conversion optimization factors

Let's go over some additional factors that help ensure conversions on your website:

Structure your navigation: On too many websites, the site navigation is cluttered and disorganized; it doesn't help drive potential customers to the pages that will give them the information they need. One of the biggest mistakes is creating site navigation that links to virtually every page on the site.

When you provide so many options, it's confusing to the visitor, and you're not taking advantage of the opportunity to lead the visitor through a page-by-page process to deliver the message you want to convey. It's like suggesting a reader jump around randomly from chapter to chapter in a novel.

No matter your site's size, try to pare your navigation down to as few elements as possible. It's okay to have a dozen links or so in your navigation, but be sure they are *organized* in a way that helps visitors easily choose the right page.

Implementing structured navigation makes it much easier for visitors to quickly find the pages that are most interesting to them.

A window covering business website doesn't have to be overly complicated. You want to make sure there's good, detailed content on every one of the pages, but that doesn't mean you need a lot of pages.

The easier you make it on the visitor, the more likely you are to get a conversion. Carefully scrutinize every part of your site and see where you can simplify the process. Of course, a good marketing firm can be a huge help in this process.

Make sure your site has a voice: If your copy sounds like every other window covering business site, you're missing an opportunity to differentiate your business from the competition.

While the tone of your website's copy should always be professional, "professional" doesn't have to mean "antiseptic."

Too many people believe that business-oriented copy needs to read like the most academic of research papers. *This is a huge mistake.*

Copy can be professional but still sound *resonant* and *personal* — even on a home improvement website.

Read through your copy and see if it sounds like you're simply having a casual conversation with a potential client. That's the tone you want. The more personal flair you can inject in your website copy, the more it will stand out from the vanilla sound of so many other window treatment business sites.

Having a unique voice gives you an edge. It tells potential clientele that you're different, and when they are choosing between you and a competitor, that might be the advantage that makes them choose you.

Provide a box that lets visitors search your site: This depends on how well your site has been developed, but if you have good, useful copy on all your pages, a "search this site" feature can be a great boon.

If you're not sure how well your site delivers results when people search for certain common terms or phrases, test its functionality yourself before letting the feature go live. A search function that works poorly is worse than no search function at all.

If you do have a great site search that gives perfect results every time, this can help visitors find specific products, features, or information quickly without having to scan a bunch of pages.

This search data can also be helpful in telling you what people are looking for, allowing you to better promote those areas. Better promotion of your services means *more conversions*.

Be consistent in formatting (fonts, bold, italics, images): There should be a consistent look and feel to all your pages, making them seem (as they are) all part of the same message.

While some homepages may look a bit different than the internal pages, it is important to be consistent from one page to the next. Your primary navigation should not change from one page to the next, nor should your footer, page layout, colors, etc.

When you don't have that kind of consistency, the onsite experience can be quite jarring, and this can ruin the experience for visitors. Any bad experience is bad for conversions.

Make sure your site is optimized for mobile: I covered this extensively earlier, but I'm just noting it again here because it's absolutely *essential* for conversions.

window covering business sites get a little more desktop traffic than some other industries do, but as we close in on 2020, you're still getting *over 50 percent of your traffic from mobile devices*.

No one using a smartphone wants to deal with an old-school website that isn't optimized for mobile. They want to call you with a single click. They want to be able to view your product lines and look over your services in a clear, easily viewed format.

If you're not optimized for mobile, you could be throwing away *half or even more* of your conversions. Remember, conversions create customers, and (of course) customers create revenue. Can you afford to just wave goodbye to all that business?

Delivering great conversion copy

I hit upon a number of content considerations earlier in this section, but let's talk a bit more about persuasive copy and how it can convert visitors into customers.

More isn't always better: Don't overload your pages with thousands of words of copy. You're trying to deliver a message, so provide just enough information to get that message across, and then get out of the way. You don't want to bury the visitor with minutiae that don't build your brand or deliver a conversion.

However... don't take that to mean that a couple of paragraphs on each page will get the job done. Your copy needs to be detailed enough that people clearly understand what you're conveying and accept you as your area's top expert on window treatments.

If you have a Frequently Asked Questions (FAQ) page, be thorough, but resist the urge to pack it with tons of salesy language. Provide honest-to-goodness answers to actual likely questions.

For the most part, keep sentences short and to the point. Don't repeat information that you've covered elsewhere on the site. (I realize that's ironic, considering how often I've doubled down and even *tripled* down on important points in this book. But there's a good reason for that.)

Your visitor's time is valuable, and digging through long stretches of copy to find necessary information will cause a visitor to look elsewhere. Everything is a balancing act: Provide strong, detailed, concise information, and then wrap it up.

Did I make it perfectly clear that you shouldn't skimp on content? Content really is king, and the higher quantity of strong content you have on your site and your pages, the higher the traffic and conversions, generally.

Content-rich sites also attract more links, which is always a good thing (presuming the links are legitimate and relevant). Be sure to have plenty of content; just make sure that the content you have is broken up into *clear, concise, easily digestible* chunks.

Show that you're trustworthy: Why don't people convert even though a site clearly shows that it can provide a definite solution to the visitor's need?

Usually, the biggest roadblock is that the site hasn't *sufficiently communicated its trustworthiness* to the visitor. I'm sure it's rare that you get a client who picked a name out of a hat for something as important as home renovation.

Because far too many bad businesspeople have promised too much and delivered too little in the digital age, online customers tend to have their shields up. They're afraid of wasting money, wasting time, putting their money on the wrong horse.

Your copy should be consistently focused on putting a potential customer's mind at ease. Certain guarantees can help with this. Testimonials (both written and especially in video, as noted earlier) can help with this.

The visitor wants to believe you. The visitor wants to benefit from what you have to offer. As the business owner, you have to conquer that concern in the visitor's mind that you might not be legitimate.

Trustworthiness, transparency, credible authority, lots of high-value content, and plain old decency: These are your best weapons.

These factors would be true of any business, but they're obviously critical for a window covering business.

People might buy some gizmo online if it's really cheap, even if they're not 100 percent sure the seller is entirely trustworthy. They might grab a burrito from a random food truck at the park if they're famished, holding out hope that it won't make them sick.

But they certainly won't work with a home improvement company they don't trust completely. It's your job to make that perfectly clear through the information you include on your website.

Everything on your site needs to show you can be trusted. Provide real contact information. Display your photograph. Include pictures of your business. Include a short video featuring you and your staff. Make visitors feel like they've already visited your location before they've even set foot in it.

If you're a Better Business Bureau member, make note of that (and display the seal). If you're affiliated with national dealers, of course you want to put their seals up there. Display positive reviews and testimonials. That's what we call **social proof**. It's a key aspect of ensuring more website conversions.

Trust, trust, trust. That's what you're selling.

Check the readability of your copy on various browsers, including mobile browsers: Nothing will run off a visitor faster than a website that's hard to read. The fonts and colors you use might look wonderful in Google Chrome but awful in Mozilla Firefox or Microsoft Edge.

Test the readability of your site in all types of browsers and select options that display clearly (and in a compelling way) across the board.

And of course, make sure the site is optimized for mobile — and that means it displays and functions well on both iPhones and Android devices.

While SEO is important, always put the human visitor first: Yes, I'll repeat myself one more time: If your copy reads like it's intended for search engine spiders and not the reader, *you're not going to convert*. This practice massively undermines your credibility and serves to confuse the reader. Get your keywords in there, but be certain that the copy in personable and conversational in tone.

Finding the balance in copy that's compelling for readers yet also keyword-rich is an art of its own, and a good internet marketing expert and copywriter can be a great help with this.

Onsite organic SEO

Effective SEO isn't simply a matter of getting your site to rank as highly as possible in SERPs or driving as much traffic as possible to your site.

You want people coming to your site who want to purchase your particular services. If the visitors who arrive aren't interested in home improvement services at this time, they're obviously not going to convert into clientele.

Effective SEO delivers the *right* people to your site, people who are likely to convert. To achieve this, you want to use relevant keyword phrases not only in the copy people read, but also in the coding of the site itself.

This requires making use of **meta tags**, which help inform the search engines of what your site is all about. Of course, appropriate use of meta tags also gives your SEO a big overall boost. Search engines are better able to index these pages, providing a big increase in visibility and rankings.

Meta tags are HTML tags you place on the coding of the page. They can include **title tags**, **description meta tags**, **heading tags** and **image tags**, among others.

Certain types of site software provide toolkits that make it easier to add these tags to your site without messing around with HTML — the most basic website programming language.

Title tags: These are extremely important indicators that inform search engines what your page is about. Things to keep in mind:

The title tag is not to be confused with your *page heading*. It's part of your meta data and the title users see at the very top of your web browser. It's also the title people will see for your site on a SERP.

Google typically only displays the first 50-60 characters in a title tag, so don't go over 60 (including spaces). Because you have a limited number of characters, your title is precious real estate. Think like a user and type in search terms you know the user will use.

Some users will only look at titles, so your title needs to be something that will compel the user to click through when your result shows up in SERPs.

Titles for each page also must be unique; they cannot be repeated anywhere else on your site. The best SEO practice is to include your keyword in your page title, preferably at the beginning of the title.

For your industry, as with all tags on your site, something specific to home improvement (and window fashions, of course) obviously should be incorporated.

Meta description tags: These describe what your page is about and are displayed along with your title in search results. Obviously, how your site is described will be a huge influence on whether a searcher clicks through to your site.

Google will display 120-158 characters (including spaces) for a meta description, so again, don't make it too long. Make it something that's direct and compelling, and include words that users are likely to use to find the page.

Get your primary keywords in there, but avoid keyword-stuffing, and also try to include a call to action such as *read more about…*, *find out…*, or *learn all about…*.

An enticing description will increase your click-through rate. It also lets you stand out from other sites that show up in SERPs.

Heading (H1) tags: These tags are intended to indicate the most prominent (and presumably most important) text on a page. These are followed by other H tags, H2 through H6, ordered from most important to least. These are important from an SEO perspective, but they also make the page easy to read.

Think about a magazine. Important things, such as the magazine's title or a front-page feature, would be in H1. A smaller article's title might be in H2 and a subtitle in H3.

Google expects a webpage to be laid out with a series of headers that makes sense to the reader. These tell Google and other search engines what is most important.

It's important not to go overboard on H1 tags, just like you don't want to go overboard on things such as bold or italics.

Emphasis is used to *differentiate* things as being more important than other things; ***if everything is "important," then nothing is***.

Abusing H1 tags will definitely get a webpage penalized by Google and other search engines, so creating multiple H1 tags on a page purely for the purpose of trying to improve your search engine ranking is definitely frowned upon. It's generally best to stick with just one H1 tag per page.

Image tags: While both human visitors and search engine spiders can interpret words on a page, images themselves are (for the most part) only able to be interpreted by actual humans.

To let the spiders know what's being seen in an image, you need to add image tags. These are also known as **alt-image tags**, because the text you include in them will be shown to your human visitors if the image fails to load for some reason.

Search engines crawl these tags as well, so by including home improvement-related keywords (when natural and appropriate) in these tags, you're once again improving your SEO for people who search for these keywords.

As usual, don't stuff keywords into tags willy-nilly, because that can blow up in your face.

An additional way to improve image SEO is by giving the image's actual file a descriptive name. Instead of something like "IMG1230.jpg" for an image showing cellular roller shades, rename the file "cellular-roller-shades-001.jpg." The hyphens allow search engines to recognize the composite parts as individual words.

Section 3:

Reviews and Reputation

CHAPTER 5
Customer Review Sites and Reputation Management

The internet lets you tell everyone in the world how awesome your services and/or products are. You can go on about your incredible customer service on your website. You can develop advertisements that boast about your being the very best home improvement company in your neighborhood or city.

And if that spiel is legitimate, worded well, and backed up by testimonials from happy customers, people will most likely accept that your assessment of your stellar reputation is genuine.

However, there's another side to dealing with reputation issues in the age of the internet:

You're not the only one who gets to weigh in on your business.

Whether you like it or not, members of the general public will have their say on their experiences with your company.

As I noted earlier, customer/client review sites exist to aggregate information from people who have tried out a business and wish to write a review.

While some people enjoy writing reviews of almost every establishment or service provider they interact with, most only take the time to write a review if they had a spectacular experience — or a truly horrible one.

For this reason, businesses need to be ready to do a great job for every customer.

That's not a bad idea in theory: With its online reputation potentially at stake every day, a business presumably will make a point of doing a great job with every customer interaction. That's extra impetus to go the extra mile, and it's better for the customers as well.

Of course, like anything else on the internet, reviews can be gamed.

As terrible as it sounds, certain less scrupulous business owners try to artificially inflate their positive reviews by registering on these sites under a variety of different names.

Even worse, these business owners often *pan* their local competitors — whether or not the criticisms are deserved — under other names.

Also, unfair reviews are sometimes posted by people who don't necessarily have a stake in the businesses. Some people just get a kick out of ripping companies — again, regardless of whether such criticism is actually warranted.

Others try to trade super-positive reviews for free stuff, discounts, upgrades, and other perks. All of these underhanded strategies can influence the legitimacy of online reviews.

Because of this, most of the major review sites, along with Google, set up algorithms that are intended to seek out and hide or remove reviews that are false or illegitimate. These algorithms have had mixed results, but they've at least applied some controls to a process that can be fraught with misbehavior.

The major sites also include some options to allow businesses to contest unfair or inappropriate reviews, and all let the business comment on reviews that appear, providing the company an opportunity to place the criticism in context and (if desired) to communicate a desire to address any legitimate concerns that were noted.

I'll talk about some of those options in a bit, but what's most important to take from this is that *you must be vigilant in reviewing your window covering business's online reputation.*

This means paying attention to whatever people are saying about your business on review sites, in blogs, in news reports, and anywhere else.

People who contract for something services related to their homes are more likely to post about the experience — whether positive or negative — than someone who simply bought a bagel from the coffee shop down the street. (Granted, there are people who do this, and we wish them all the best.)

If a reviewer hits you with a particularly negative review, it's *critical* that you not let it sit out there without any comment or response. If several bad reviews go un-answered, that can be *extraordinarily damaging* to your reputation. No one wants to contract for services with a window covering business that's been shredded in online reviews.

Remember at the start of this book when I explained how more and more people every day are getting information about local businesses from their smartphones?

These devices make it unbelievably easy to quickly check out reviews when a potential customer pulls up your Google listing or a Yelp app. And remember, Bing also integrates Yelp reviews into its searches.

These days, when someone simply clicks on your business in a maps application or does a search for nearby businesses and comes across yours, those reviews are sitting right there to be read.

No matter how well you promote your window covering business, if several negative reviews pop up any time someone check you out, your business is in big trouble.

You absolutely *can't afford to ignore online customer reviews*. Good ones can be incredibly helpful, but bad ones can be devastating.

You *must* proactively generate positive online reviews. They're critical for business success.

Before we go any further, we need to talk about:

Review Gating

I mentioned this very briefly in an earlier chapter, but let's take a moment to dig in deeper.

Review gating refers to the process of using specialized software to filter out potential negative reviews and only let people publish positive reviews of your business.

The typical process works like this: You send an email to a customer (asking whether they were satisfied with the services you provided and whether they'd like to publish a review.

If they were completely satisfied, they're guided to a clickable link where they can easily write a quick review.

If they were *not* entirely satisfied, they're guided to clickable link that lets them contact you directly about their concerns — bypassing the publishing process.

Obviously, this let businesses avoid negative reviews by "heading them off at the pass." Which is why Google banned the practice in 2018.

You don't want to be involved in this, because as I noted before, the last thing you want to do is upset Google. If you get caught, you'll be penalized.

With that said, there *are* software options that allow people to publish negative reviews is they wish, but they *also* provide the option to reach out to the business first.

By doing this, a dissatisfied client has the opportunity to address concerns before reviewing, if so desired, but is not actually barred from leaving a negative review.

We've found that many homeowners are fine with contacting a home improvement business directly before leaving a negative review, and after working things out, they either choose not to leave a negative review —

or actually leave a positive one! At RRM, we have proprietary software that facilitates this process.

If a marketing agency claims it can make all of your negative reviews disappear or entirely block them from occurring, don't work with that business. No one can legitimately promise that.

However, there are means by which you can negotiate with people who have left negative reviews and often get them to remove the review or even choose to modify it to be more positive. Also, all review platforms have processes for removing truly fake reviews.

At RRM, while there's never a guarantee, we have an excellent success rate at getting many negative reviews removed or replaced with more positive reviews.

While there are lots of review sites online — some of which exist only to cover particular types of businesses or niches — here are the main players:

Yelp

Google reviews have cut into Yelp's dominance a bit, but the latter remains the big daddy (or big mommy, take your pick) of review sites.

As one of the first sites to marry local search, user reviews, and social networking aspects, it's grown astronomically since its founding in 2004, and its reach has expanded with ridiculous speed in recent years. As of December 2018, Yelp had accumulated *177 million unique reviews*.

Yelp also has a reputation system that lets visitors see which contributing users are the most popular, respected, and prolific. This can help visitors judge how legitimate reviews from these users tend to be, among other things.

Business owners can also communicate with contributors who post reviews on their page through messages or public comments.

Having reviews of your window covering business on Yelp — especially positive reviews — is a boon. That's been true since the site launched, but it's especially true now.

As I mentioned earlier, the idea of a review aggregation site compiling plaudits and criticisms of various businesses is a controversial one.

Some business owners have questioned Yelp's own credibility, especially after allegations emerged that some Yelp salespeople might have offered to hide negative reviews of businesses that paid for advertising sponsorship contracts. Yelp has refuted these allegations, but they're pervasive enough to be concerning.

Certain businesses also question the effectiveness of Yelp's review filter, which is intended to prevent and remove illegitimate reviews. In certain cases, the businesses claim, reviews that would seem to be clearly false show up next to "real" reviews. In others, honest-to-goodness legit reviews get snagged by the filter and are not displayed.

In the same way that Google won't disclose the specifics of its search ranking algorithms to prevent them from being gamed, Yelp won't disclose the specifics of its review filter algorithms.

Several class-action lawsuits have been filed against Yelp by businesses that have had positive reviews removed but have been unable to get negative reviews similarly redressed.

The fundamental allegation in most of these suits is that Yelp is trying to force businesses to advertise (which is how Yelp makes its money). However, as of this writing, there have been no court decisions proving or even suggesting that Yelp has acted inappropriately.

One frustrating factor with Yelp is that it no longer allows businesses to directly solicit reviews. It wants satisfied clients to decide entirely on their own to review a business.

I don't recommend trying to work around this regulation, because if Yelp catches you soliciting reviews, it can penalize your home improvement business on its platform.

With that said, there's nothing wrong with asking satisfied customers for reviews in general, and if *they* ask whether to do so Yelp, there's nothing prohibiting you from saying "that's fine."

Advertising with Yelp: While the company continues to contend that advertising with Yelp won't affect the display of organically created user reviews (either positive or negative), it seems safe to assume that advertising on Yelp can't hurt.

At the very least, the company makes no bones about the fact that your Yelp page will be better promoted and get more visibility if you're an advertiser.

However, that increased visibility might not be worth the return on investment for most small businesses. Many marketing experts believe Yelp's paid ads currently cost far more than what you receive in return.

The numbers can get a little confusing if you're not familiar with **cost per impressions**, which is the model Yelp uses for the ads. Much like traditional advertising, an *impression* merely means that someone has *seen* your ad. You're paying for the ad regardless of whether someone clicks through to your site.

Cost per click, by comparison, only costs you money if someone clicks through.

With Yelp ads, the cost per impression (CPM) is exponentially more expensive than it is with standard CPM advertising. It's also much harder to track how effective your advertising is when you can't get click-through numbers.

Yelp is also requiring a one-year commitment for its most favorable rates, which aren't particularly low in the first place.

In general, I don't recommend Yelp advertising at this time for most small businesses, including window treatment companies. If you have plenty of extra marketing money to burn and want to give it a shot, it's an option to consider. But I think you'll get better ROI from other initiatives.

Google reviews / Google My Business

I covered GMB extensively earlier, so I won't get into it deeply here.

In the previous edition of this book, I went on about how GMB worked with Google+ and Google Places and...well, you know how all that turned out.

The thing to know here is that people can review your business through Google, and these reviews are incredibly important. With the vast majority of people using Google to research local businesses, these reviews are among the most prominently displayed to users.

The quality *and* quantity of Google reviews your business receives also plays an indirect role in SEO. The short version is that Google's spiders can tell which businesses are reviewed a lot, so they grant those websites more authority. And more authority means higher search rankings.

Note that if you haven't verified your window covering business with GMB yet, your information won't necessarily show up on Maps, Search, and other Google services. Additionally, *only verified businesses can respond to reviews*.

So if you're not sure whether you've gone through verification, stop everything (seriously, just put this book down or close your e-reader) and do it right now.

Google systems are integrated by default into all Android-based devices, so you want to have the best reviews possible on your Google listing.

When someone Googles your business, your verified GMB listing typically will appear on the right side of the SERP. One of the first things people will see is your Google review rating: your overall score (on a five-star scale) and how many reviews you've received.

While it's great to have a handful of five-star reviews, surveys have shown that it's actually better to have a *higher quantity* of reviews, even if they're not all five stars!

In other words, people generally have greater trust in a business that has (for example) 25 reviews with a 4.7 overall rating than one that has seven reviews with a perfect five-star rating.

You always want five-star reviews, of course, but don't let "perfect be the enemy of the good," as they say. Work hard to generate *a lot* of Google reviews.

Like Yelp, Google My Business uses a reviewer algorithm to ensure the display of the most legitimate reviews.

Google provides an option to flag reviews as inappropriate if they violate its guidelines, but as with Yelp, it can be hard to simply have a negative review removed if it falls within the guidelines. You can respond to a negative review with comments to provide your side of the issue.

Angie's List: pros and cons of advertising

Angie's List is well known for providing user-based reviews on a number of business, often those related to contractors, but it lists window covering businesses as well.

If you haven't heard of it, the idea is pretty simple: It acts as a review/recommendation site for various contractors, businesses, and services. In that sense, it's like Yelp and similar review sites, but Angie's List has a more complex methodology, one that is likely to produce reviews that are more accurate because they're more clearly verifiable.

For much of its existence, Angie's List was purely a paid membership site. In July 2016, it became a "freemium" service.

This means that people can access more than 10 million reviews through the free basic membership tier. Paid subscriptions (at "Gold" and "Silver" levels) provide additional functionality.

As of late 2018, Angie's List said its membership included 6 million households and 720 categories of local service providers, with about 60,000 reviews submitted to the site every month.

Angie's List also has stringent requirements for businesses listed on the site. You can create a profile for your business for free, but you supposedly cannot pay to be listed or necessarily increase your ranking purely through a paid sponsorship.

Angie's List advertising options: Angie's List knows it has a winning pitch just in the demographics of its members: According the the company, most users are college graduates and have an average household income of $100,000. That's an impressively prequalified group to whom you can market your window treatment sales and installation services.

Angie's List offers a few options for advertising. There's traditional advertising that can be done on the site, in the company's monthly publication, or through the company's call center.

(Angie's List claims that listed businesses that also advertise on the site, in general, receive more than 10 times the number of inquiries from members.)

Angie's List member experiences: How effective advertising on Angie's List can be is obviously affected by its member base and those members' experiences. While many Angie's List members have reported very good experiences with the services, it's not hard to find members who have been less impressed, or even openly criticize the service.

Most of the concerns expressed do not seem to be about the quality of the reviews themselves, though some critics have questioned how objective Angie's List can be when it's accepting advertising from businesses, and others have noted that a number of categories on the site are pretty sparse when it comes to reviews.

The biggest issues with the user experience seem to depend on how tolerant you are of Angie's List interactions. The company regularly sends out emails with offers from advertising businesses, which can be taken as spam by many individuals.

It also sends out occasional automated calls for feedback and to solicit member reviews. Some people understandably consider this far more intrusive than the occasional email.

In addition, some former members have complained that the only membership options are to pay for a full year or be locked into a monthly auto-renewal process that the service makes it tricky to cancel.

How does this affect you as a potential advertiser? Well, if Angie's List is sending out your ads in a fashion that members find annoying or even obnoxious, it's going to be hard for the members to divorce themselves from that connotation in their minds.

The site's credibility wasn't helped by a class-action suit filed on behalf of Angie's List members. The suit claims that Angie's List automatically renews membership fees at a higher rate than customers are led to believe, calling the practice a "systematic and repeated breach of its membership agreement." In 2014, the company paid $2.8 million to settle a lawsuit regarding the claims.

If Angie's List continues to gain a poor online reputation in some places — which is obviously ironic for an online contractor reputation service — you might want to consider whether you want your window covering business linked to theirs in your customers' minds.

Angie's List Advertiser Experiences: As with member experiences, you'll find a broad variety of opinions on whether advertising on Angie's List has proved valuable for local businesses. Some claim great experiences, finding a pool of motivated buyers that easily converts interested parties into clientele.

Others claim the return on investment just hasn't been there, especially when you balance it with what many business owners consider fairly intrusive pushes by Angie's List customer reps.

Ultimately, it appears that whether your advertising is largely successful for you or not, either way you'll have to be able to live with the hard sell from Angie's List.

Here are a few things to consider:

- **Is your service likely to get solid reviews in general?** There's little point to advertising on a review/referral site if members who see your ads and click through don't like what they see when they get there. If you're definitely at the top of your game — and your customers agree — it makes sense to raise your profile on a review/referral-based site.

- **Are you already getting regularly leads and conversions from your free listing on Angie's List?** Advertising might increase that to some degree, but you'll likely either be locked into a lengthy commitment or pay full freight to find out. Can your window covering business afford that?

- **Is your current advertising/marketing already reaching the Angie's List demographic in your area?** With only so many marketing dollars at your disposal, you don't want your efforts to overlap unless there's very good reason for it.

There's no question that Angie's List has steadily become an influential force in local businesses and services, but how that's going to pan out in either the short or long term is very much in question.

There's no shortage of strong opinions on the service, ranging from extremely positive to just as negative. The class-action suit is also a big red flag for a company that's built on the concept of promoting highly reputable businesses.

Garnering more reviews

While negative reviews obviously are bad for your business, the best way to counter them typically is to solicit reviews from satisfied customers. They're obviously far more likely to rate your business positively, and as I noted before, the quantity of reviews your business receives will provide a huge boost to your rankings in local search results.

Like it or not, there's no way to get rid of online reviews. They're simply a reality of the times. So instead of fighting them, do your best to get the largest quantity of great reviews you can. Ways to do this include:

Solicit reviews on your website: I mentioned before that Yelp prohibits businesses from directly soliciting reviews, so don't do that. However, there's nothing wrong with asking satisfied customers to review you on other platforms.

You can create a page on your site specifically intended for reviews, and that can have a simple form they can fill out. The easier you make it for the customer, the more likely you are to get a review — particularly a positive one.

Add a review request to invoices and receipts: While putting the request on a printed form isn't as user-friendly as other methods, because the customer will have to then go online to do the review, it's a good complementary option. Also, if you use digital invoices or receipts, those can include a link your customer can use to easily go straight to filling out a review.

Put it in an email: Again, including a simple link to your own review form or that on a popular platform (such as your page, Yelp, Angie's List, etc.) makes it easy for the customer. Just be sure you're being careful not to spam your customers with emails, which could very easily prompt *negative* reviews.

Monitoring and responding to positive and negative reviews

It's never fun having your services criticized, regardless of whether the feedback is fair. When it comes to an online review, the impact of a complaining customer is far heavier than that of a card in a customer feedback box. It can imperil your business now and in the future.

This is why it's so critical to stay on top of how your business is being reviewed online. Remember that *reviews are good* for your business in many ways, so you shouldn't just put your head in the sand or take actions to stay under the radar. You do a good job, and your customers know this. The key is to get them to make this known, as I discussed in the previous section.

One thing you absolutely must do is *monitor all reviews you receive*. It's not as hard as it sounds. In fact, there are services available that can help monitor all the major review sites and let you review them together, and your internet marketing professional can help with this. If you don't know what's being said about you online, you're powerless to adapt to it.

While it's most important to respond (and respond *quickly*) to negative reviews, the importance of responding to positive reviews is often overlooked.

When people take the time to say something nice about your company, they like to know that you've seen the review and appreciate it. Thanking them and promising to do a great job will go a long way toward attracting new clientele.

Also, if the only reviews you respond to are the negative ones, that leaves a poor impression on everyone who sees that page. Thanking people for glowing reviews and responding positively to critical reviews will always paint you in the very best light.

Granted, it can be challenging at first to find a positive tone in replying to a negative review, but it's not too hard once you get used to it.

After a cooling-off period, respond privately to the reviewer: You don't always have to start off with a public comment. On Yelp, for example, you can reach out to the critical customer first through a private message. Perhaps the criticism resulted purely from a misunderstanding or miscommunication that can be worked out.

Whatever the case, give yourself a little time to let your emotions ebb. It's natural to be upset by a negative review, but resist the temptation to overreact.

Instead, take a deep breath and evaluate the customer's complaint. Determine what has been (or can still be) done to address the issue. Engage the customer with a short and positive private response — either through the online review platform or via email — that recognizes the customer's criticism and discusses ways to remedy the situation.

By taking the issue offline, you can prevent a potentially ugly back-and-forth discussion that could draw even more unwanted attention to the review. If successful in resolving the issue offline, you can politely ask the customer to revise the review to note that the complaint was addressed or even delete it altogether.

If that doesn't help, provide a public reply: Even if you work things out privately, the reviewer might not elect to revise or remove the original negative review. Don't badger the reviewer; this might only lead the reviewer to further criticize your company on a follow-up comment or another review.

If you believe the issue was resolved, note that you reached out and successfully addressed the customer's concern. You might also include what steps you took to ensure satisfaction — for example, that a discount was offered or a replacement product provided.

If you believe there were legitimate inaccuracies with claims made in the review, offer a short response that corrects the facts. Again, keep it positive and professional. Maintaining the high road and appearing conciliatory to customer concerns is more important than establishing "your side."

Another thing to consider is that you should do everything in your power to discourage negative reviews in the first place (while encouraging positive ones). The foundation of this is simple: Do great work, provide great customer service, and generally make everyone who works with you feel happy and satisfied.

However, no matter how well your business is run, there will always be customers who are unhappy with the product or service provided.

That's just the nature of business and the broad spectrum by which people interpret their customer experience. Some people are easy to please; others never seem to be satisfied. Two people could have the exact same experience and interpret it two completely different ways.

Customers who are unsatisfied often turn to online review sites to voice their frustration. Some wish to warn potential customers about your practices, some want to damage your company's reputation out of spite, and some hope to receive a response that could include an invitation to revisit the work or provide a discount or refund.

Many times, the customer will note concerns directly with a business before choosing to post them publicly. It's critical to seize this opportunity while you still have a chance to allay these concerns. Respond quickly and work out a resolution before a negative review is posted.

In most instances, staying positive, reassuring the customer that concerns will be addressed, and reaching some sort of compromise — even if that requires a rebate, refund, or other concession — is far preferable to the negative word of mouth a negative online review can generate.

Over time, these reviews can cost you much more than what would be involved in proactively remedying a customer's complaint.

CHAPTER 6
Email Marketing

Think about the most tech-wary person you know, a true technophobe through and through.

Can you think of anyone? Someone who has truly let the digital revolution pass him by. Doesn't have a smartphone, much less the two (or even three) some people carry today. Doesn't have a laptop, much less a tablet. Has no interest in Twitter, doesn't care about Facebook, wouldn't know Yelp from yogurt.

At the very least, your friend almost certainly has a home PC and uses email.

In reality, almost everyone in America uses email and checks it regularly. Even people who rarely leave home check their email on a constant basis.

Most modern email systems provide pop-ups and alerts to let you know you have a new email. Preschoolers have it. Great-grandmothers have it. With postal rates continuing to rise all the time, people continue to shift from communicating by snail mail to email.

And even if you don't own or use a smartphone, it's a fair bet your mobile phone — even one manufactured a decade or more ago — has the capability to receive and send email. Your email provider is most likely free to use, making it all the more valuable. Email access is easy, it's free, it's omnipresent.

Of course, email also produces a lot of spam, which is another thing entirely, but I'll get back to that.

Email marketing can be tricky in some ways, but it's a marketing initiative no business can afford to ignore. You have a free way to communicate with your prospective customers who opt-in to your emails.

Can emails sometimes get lost in the morass of communications people get in their inboxes every day? Sure, but no less than direct mail advertising gets lost in the stack of junk that piles up in the mailbox. And direct mail costs *money*.

Email is by far the most cost-effective way to deliver marketing messages for your window covering business. You can send personalized, targeted, and interest-specific messages to a large number of people.

But there are other advantages. You can include links in email that prompt the recipient to click through directly to your site/landing page. Also, studies show that more than 80 percent of the email you send is opened in the first 48 hours after delivery, so you can get a fairly immediate response or action based on it.

First, avoid spam

Before getting into some email strategies, let me repeat something I touched on earlier:

Never spam.

Never, *ever* spam.

If you're sending out a mass email you think *might* be spam, it's almost certainly spam. Don't send it.

Sending out unsolicited emails is the very best way to get your business identified as a spammer, ensuring your emails a permanent grave in the ever-more-sensitive spam filters developed by Gmail, Yahoo mail, Hotmail/Outlook, etc.

When was the last time you even *checked* your spam filter, much less actually clicked on something you didn't recognize in it?

Spam emails are typically automatically deleted every 30 days or so for good reason: They're not beneficial, and no one wants them.

Even if your unsolicited email sneaks around the filter and reaches a recipient's inbox, most email providers provide a one-click method to report an email as spam. If your email looks spammy, you can expect this to happen.

Oh, and one other thing:

Spamming is technically illegal.

So there's that.

Sticking with professional email standards keeps your emails legally compliant and ensures great relationships with the people who receive your emails.

An internet marketing professional can help you understand all the ways your email could be classified as spam, though they mostly fall under common sense. Even if you always send emails to people who have opted in, there are two critical things to consider:

To send commercial emails that don't violate the law, every email should include two things: the *physical address* associated with your business (a P.O. box is accepted as long as it's associated with your business's actual location), and an *unsubscribe option*.

The unsubscribe process also has to be accomplishable by replying to a single email or by visiting a single web page.

You're also required by law to remove anyone who unsubscribes from your email list permanently within 10 days of the unsubscribe request. You can't add that person back without the recipient's explicit permission.

Getting permission

If you haven't received permission from a recipient, your email almost certainly will be considered spam. So always get permission.

Technically, there are two types of permission: **implicit** or **explicit**.

Implicit permission occurs when someone shares his or her email address with you for some reason, such as filling out a contact form on your website for more information regarding a particular service or item.

That's opened the door for you to contact the person for that reason, but you haven't actually asked permission to continue to contact the person down the line with product offers and the like (unless that's clearly noted when the person signs on).

It's much safer to get explicit permission: Tell the person what to expect when by providing an email. If you plan to send promotions and other communications, be straight about it.

Once you've compiled your list (more on that in a moment), don't share it, don't sell it, don't trade it. Those are surefire ways to destroy your reputation with your customers.

Do I really have to be that careful? In a word, yes. As few as two spam complaints per 1,000 customers can prompt internet service providers to block you from sending emails to their customers.

Even when you've received explicit permission, your emails can be interpreted as spam depending on how they're constructed or how often you send them.

In a sense, it doesn't matter whether the recipient asked you to email in the first place. If the emails appear too frequently, don't appear legitimate, or don't provide useful information, they can soon be interpreted to be spam.

Putting your list together

It's harder these days to compile a large list than it used to be, which is understandable: People are more careful about giving out their email address for fear of getting crushed by communications every day. Ever overlook an important email because it was buried in a bunch of inbox chaff? It's not a fun feeling.

In reality, you don't need a huge list for your email marketing to be effective.

The best lists contain the names of loyal repeat customers, referral sources who respect others' privacy, and interested prospects who know you and your business well enough to recognize (and want) your communications. Ultimately, *quality* is much more important than *quantity*.

Unless your list is going to be extremely short, it's best to use some sort of database (or software specifically designed to organize emails and contacts).

The database for your email list can be part of a customer database you currently use, or it can be something entirely separate. That said, it's *critical* not to get confused about which customers (and prospective customers) have agreed to receive emails from you.

A contact form on your website is one of the most common ways to compile an email list. If you're having trouble getting visitors to fill out the form, some incentives can help: *Join our email list and receive 20 percent off your first purchase.*

Design a great email

An effective email starts with the header. This includes the "From" line and address and the subject line.

The "From" line doesn't simply have to be your email address per se. You can set this up to read as your full name, or your company name, or both.

If another name (such as your website domain) might be more recognizable to people who have signed up for your emails, it's best to use this name. You don't want recipients to be confused about who's sending them emails.

The **subject line** is incredibly important, because this is the most information that will be provided before someone opens your email. It must compel the recipient to want to know more.

Subject line real estate is valuable, because most email providers only display the first 30 to 50 characters, and most mobile devices only show the first 20 to 30 characters. You need to get your point across concisely.

As with any professional communication, it's critical to spell words in your subject lines correctly and avoid spammy elements such as excessive punctuations (especially exclamation points), all-caps, capitalizing the first letter of every word, or using "Re:" (when it's not actually in response to anything).

Also, ambiguous or deceptive subject lines such as "Hi!" or "I've missed you" should be avoided.

Be sure to brand your emails with a consistent template or a consistent color scheme. Including your company's logo also is a must. It should look like what it is: a professional communication from a professional provider of window treatment services.

Visual elements: Marketing pros will tell you there are a lot of psychological elements you can use in your design to draw the eye where you want it to be. That's absolutely true, but it's beyond the scope of this book.

You should know the basics: Be sure the email is clear and easy to read. Be sure the most important aspects (particularly the call to action) are eye-catching and direct. Add visual anchors such as images (within reason) to break up the copy and make it appealing to read.

(Note on images: Without getting too technical, it's much better for your images to be referenced to a remote folder than embedded. Emails with embedded links are much more likely to be filtered as junk. A marketing expert can help you understand the difference.)

Content of your email

Be personable: As with your landing page copy, you don't want to sound too academic. Talk to your recipient the same way you'd talk to a visitor to your window treatment business. Be professional, but you honestly don't have to be stuffy.

You want to contract with this person for home improvement services, and you're explaining why it will be beneficial to that person. Do so in a professional but friendly way.

Links: If you're not linking to your landing page or a page that's specific to your offer in your email, you're wasting a great opportunity. Even if your email is purely communicative, there's no reason not to provide a one-click opportunity to get more information on you and your business in the body of the email.

Use incentives: Every time you send an email, it should have a purpose. "Hey, I'm still here!" is not a purpose. Show your appreciation for people on your email list by offering them, for example, a limited-time discount on certain services. They're opening up their email boxes to you, so reward them for that.

An informational email works well, too: Maybe you're not looking to promote a particular service at this time. That's fine. Is there some information about home renovation that would be (truly) interesting to your potential clientele? If so, that's enough reason for an email.

Don't waste people's time by sending these out constantly or for minor matters, but delivering useful information is a great way to stay in people's minds, along with a great excuse to include links to your website.

If you don't have the time or resources to create your own emails, there are lots of great copywriting services that can help you achieve your goals, and many are very reasonable.

Monitoring your email results

Again, I won't get into all the technical aspects here, but there are great services that will allow you to easily track your return on investment from business emails. They let you review lots of useful data, including:

- Which emails bounced
- Why they bounced
- Who opened the emails
- What links the recipient clicked
- Who unsubscribed
- Who forwarded your emails

This data can go a long way toward helping you refine your email marketing efforts and improving conversions.

There are more elements to successful email campaigns, but understanding these basics will help you determine the best way to use email to help your business succeed.

Email lists: Should you purchase them? (Spoiler alert: no.)

A precompiled email list sure sounds like a good deal when you're markcting your window treatment business. You have a list of emails for people who are prequalified to be interested window treatment replacements or new installations. What could go wrong?

Um… just *everything*.

The first thing to remember is that even if you worked with an email list provider for a list that has been shaped to include only customers who meet certain demographic or psychographic (personality, interests, lifestyles, etc.) standards, *it's not really an opt-in list.*

No one opted in for communications regarding your services. The people on that email list simply opted in to an email communication from someone at some point in time (like the list provider).

When you're emailing people who haven't shown an interest in your business, that's something most people consider spamming — and you're not likely to see much return on those communications anyway.

Also, there's really no such thing as a good email list that's for sale. Typically, any addresses that once had value already have been spammed by a variety of other businesses.

Yes, there's that word again: **spam**.

We're printing it in bold, even though we rarely do that (extra tip: use emphasis tools such as bold sparingly so they don't lose all meaning), because it's so important to understand that contacting people through a *purchased* email list almost always equates to spam.

Again, note the word "purchased" in that previous paragraph. A list you develop yourself is different; when you *purchase* the list, that's when you get into trouble.

If your business is defined as a spammer, your email deliverability and the reputation of your IP address almost certainly will be harmed. Organizations dedicated to combating email spam have a tool called a **honeypot**.

It's a planted email address that, when emailed, identifies the sender as a spammer.

There are other spam traps that identify if an email
address is old (or no longer valid) but still receives consistent traffic.

There are effective ways to build email lists through
proper means. For the sake of your business and its reputation, don't go the purchased email route. The rewards
are few and the risks are far too great.

Section 4:

Monitoring and

Measuring

CHAPTER 7
What Gets Measured Gets Done

Yes, "What gets measured gets done." It's a well-known saying, and properly so: it works. When you're constantly monitoring and measuring your results, you can determine what's working and what's not. You can find the places where you need to revise, tweak, or even go in an entirely new direction.

Here's the beautiful thing about today's digital world: Monitoring and measuring your marketing efforts is now incredibly fast, unbelievably precise, and unexpectedly easy.

Not only that, but you have far more flexibility now in what you do with the information you get from your analytics. You'll know what you need to do and be able to do exactly that on the fly.

You can make changes to your window treatment website that go live immediately. (Yes, it can take some time for spiders to crawl the site, but changes you make will be seen by human visitors right away.)

You can revise a PPC ad so that leads see the new information the very same day. When your analytics show that your customers are excited about a particular promotion, you can showcase it on social media.

Google Analytics

This is the best known and most popular of the user-friendly measuring tools, owing at least in part to the fact that so many businesses use Google advertising and other services.

In essence, Google Analytics generates detailed statistics about a website's traffic and traffic sources, along with measuring conversions and sales. This makes it an incredibly useful tool for marketers and business owners. The basic service is free, but there's a premium option available for a fee.

The service can track visitors from a broad variety of sources, including search engines, social networks, direct visits, and referring sites. It also displays advertising, pay-per-click networks, email marketing, and digital collateral such as links within PDF documents.

Google Analytics is completely integrated with Google Ads, making it easy to review online campaigns by tracking landing page quality and conversions.

Target goals can include sales, lead generation, viewing a specific page, or downloading a particular file, among other options.

Some of the many things you can analyze

Whether you use Google Analytics or another site-monitoring tool — the former is practically a requirement, and other tools are best used in combination with Google Analytics — here are some of the many things you can monitor:

- **Number of visits**

- **Number of people who actually visited your site:** A person may visit your site more than once, and each time, that's a separate visit.

- **Number of pages per visit:** Each time a person visits your site, the visitor might view a single page or go on to view dozens of them. (If you've populated your site with great content, hopefully the visitor is reviewing it in detail.) The greater the number of pages viewed per visit, the more people are actually exploring the information it contains.

- **List of most visited pages:** This indicates the number of visits received by each individual page. You can then use this list to analyze which themes, products, and information grab your customers' attention the most. It also includes your campaign landing pages, providing you with final statistics for each of your marketing initiatives.

- **Length of stay:** This indicates how long on average your visitors stayed on your site, thus indicating how well they relate to your content. The longer your visitors stay, the greater their interest. This gets to the issue of **bounce rate**, which I'll touch on in a moment.

- **Origin of visitors:** This identifies what site someone was viewing on the internet immediately before visiting your site. Think of it like a flight: One city's airport is the place of departure; the other is the place of arrival. It's beneficial to know where your visitor arrived from — that makes it much easier to know what prompted them to check out your business.

- These origin statistics can show **direct visits**, in which customers enter your URL directly into the browser; **site referrals**, in which a visitor comes to your site after clicking on a link at another website, a **blog** or **social media network**; and **search engine results pages ("SERPs")**.

<u>Tracking phone calls</u>

Businesses that mostly do e-commerce and sell products and services online aren't so concerned with phone calls. They do the vast majority of their business digitally.

In fact, many products are sold online without any direct involvement by the person selling them. An automated purchasing system is set up, the customer purchases the item, and it's automatically delivered digitally (if not a physical item) or goes into a queue to be delivered from a drop-shipper or wholesaler.

For a business such as yours, of course, it's an entirely different story. While you certainly get inquiries by email or through a form on your website, many inquiries for window covering services come in over the phone.

Sure, some hair salons have online registration systems, just like restaurants have online reservations (either on their own site or through an app such as Open Table) and many other service providers.

As of early 2020, millennials are _far more comfortable_ handling their business _digitally_ than they are over the phone. But when looking at _all_ demographics, even today most people making an appointment with a local business do so over the phone. (Of course, there's also Skype, videoconferencing and other types of real-time chat, but I'll stick with the basics here.)

This is why understanding how to track phone calls that originate from your window covering website is so important.

Many people now make phone calls simply by clicking on a link. When they do it on a desktop computer, typically they have it set up to call through Skype or some other VoIP (**voice over Internet Protocol**) service.

These days, however, many more people will be visiting your website — or your Google My Business page, or your Yelp listing, your Facebook Business page, a PPC ad, etc. — on a digital device that's *also* a phone.

Because your phone number is also a link that allows people to call you with a click, they can contact you *immediately* directly from your listing. The easier you make it for the lead to contact you, the better.

That's why having a *clickable* phone number (just like a clickable email address) everywhere you have an internet presence is so important.

When your phone number is clickable, an experienced internet marketing pro can easily track phone calls made from your site and listings. You can see how many leads are coming directly from your site in the form of phone calls (emails also are easily tracked, as you might assume).

You can see what times of the day the site is most effective in getting phone leads, how long people visited the site before calling, what page they were viewing before they called, and so on. This lets you optimize your site to convert the most traffic into leads.

Bounce rate and site engagement

As I indicated earlier, as we close in on 2020, your website can't merely exist because "everybody has one." It's not just there to display some elegant pictures of your window treatment company, along with some basic contact information.

Your website needs to be *actively engaging* its visitors. It must be designed to communicate trustworthiness, engage the visitor, sell the visitor that you're the best solution to a particular problem, and convert the visitor into a customer.

You can implement all the best practices toward creating an engaging, high-converting site, but only through analytics will you know how well it's working — and which aspects of the site are delivering the conversions (and which are not).

The first thing most experts focus on when assessing site engagement is the **bounce rate**. Though the definition for this can vary a bit, I'll stick with the Google Analytics definition: It's the percentage of visits in which the visitor only views *one page* before leaving the site.

For certain businesses, having a high bounce rate isn't a terrible thing; they might be trying to communicate something very simple with a very basic single landing page. They might not even have more than one page on the site. That's probably true of many of your local competitors' sites, and it might be true of yours.

Bounce rate can be broken down in many ways, including factoring which visitor origins have the highest bounce rate and which have the lowest.

The other concern regarding bounce rates relates to SEO: Google and other search engines take your bounce rate into account when ranking you. It's another key reason to design your site in a way that invites the visitor to stick around and check out additional content.

Reducing bounce rate

If you've set up your site in a legitimate manner with white-hat SEO, and at least spread some solid content across several pages, you don't have to worry about the worst bounce rate percentages.

Those terrible numbers typically are reserved for sites that attract visitors through misleading (black-hat) means.

They persuade people to click through to the site by implying there is a diamond in the stocking when they click through, but what the visitor finds is a lump of coal. The visitor immediately clicks out of the site, which is why bounce rate is such a major factor in search engine rankings.

Still, the better the bounce rate, the better for your business. Ways to improve your bounce rate include:

Browser/mobile compatibility: If your site isn't optimized for mobile devices, you'll get *a lot* of bounces from visitors trying to access it on phones. Also, be sure your site displays properly on all the major browsers — especially Google Chrome, the industry leader.

Pay off your ads on your site: When someone reads an ad that promises one thing, but clicks through to discover another, that's a quick bounce. Be sure your site is set up logically and intuitively, and be sure it delivers exactly what your ads promise.

Don't annoy the visitor: If you hit the visitor with overly aggressive pop-up ads, obnoxious chat windows, and more right on the landing page, kiss that visitor goodbye. A window treatment site with a tacky interface is going to put off potential clientele in no time flat.

Keep your landing page attractive and welcoming. Let the visitor feel "at home" and interested in exploring before placing demands. It never hurts to think of a virtual visitor as a guest in your home. You can use some pop-ups to catch attention, but keep them thoughtful and relatively subtle.

Check your page load times: If your site uses extremely complicated design or lots of graphics, some pages could take a while to load — this is a known factor in high bounce rates.

You can test page load times through analytics. If your pages are taking substantially longer than average, it's time to do some redesign.

There are ways to streamline the mobile version of your site so that large files, for example, do not automatically display.

The visitor can be provided an option to display these files if desired, which might be the case, for example, if the visitor is viewing the site on a tablet or large-display smartphone over Wi-Fi.

Improve your content: This is a general tip, but it's one of the most important. Small things such as spelling and grammatical errors can cause a visitor to lose faith in your business and bounce out. So can something that could be considered polarizing, such as political statement. High-quality content returns low bounce rates. Low-quality content returns high bounce rates.

The five basic traffic metrics

When analyzing your site's traffic, there are five basic metrics to understand:

Sessions: A session is another word for a single visit. It's one person visiting your site any one time. If someone visits your site 15 times, those visits count as 15 sessions, whether she stayed on the site for 5 minutes or 50.

Unique visitors: A unique visitor is one person visiting your site any number of times during a defined period. If someone visits your site eight times in a week, that person still counts as one unique visitor.

Page views: A single page view is any one visitor viewing one page of your site, one time. The page must have a unique address (URL). If someone visits your landing page and then clicks a link to your About Us page, those are *two* page views.

Time on site: This is the total amount of time one visitor spends on your site in the course of a single session. Average time on site is a critical measure of visit quality and visitor interest.

Referrers: If someone clicks a search result link to reach your site, the point of origin — the departure airport I talked about earlier — is known as the referrer.

There are many ways in which a marketing professional can use these metrics to help improve your site's traffic and conversions, but the details go somewhat beyond the scope of this book.

What's critical to understand regarding monitoring and measuring is the digital age lets you precisely understand every aspect of your site's effectiveness and your marketing campaign — and it lets you make virtually instantaneous changes to optimize your efforts.

Knowing which referrers tend to send the most traffic your way can help you decide where to focus your marketing and promotional efforts.

Of course, it's just as important to know how well visitors are converting who arrive from particular referrers — another statistic that can be easily mined from the data.

Analytics essentially provide you honest feedback on all your efforts. People might tell you they like one thing or another, but the proof is in how long they spend on a page, what they choose to click on, whether they decide to move forward and convert to a customer. The digital age lets you see all that information in a way that can power your success.

Section 5:

Working with a

Marketing Professional

CHAPTER 8
Finding a Qualificd, Principled
(Internet) Marketing Professional

You know why I put internet in parentheses: Because as I've noted several times before, internet marketing is virtually synonymous with marketing as we enter 2020 and move forward.

However, many marketers remain behind the 8-ball when it comes to understanding how to promote their companies online.

You'll want to find a company that specializes in online marketing, but it's just as important to be sure the company uses appropriate methods that will keep you on the good side of Google, other search engines, and laws regarding spam and legitimate marketing methods.

But this consideration is most important of all: You want to work with **full-stack marketing agency**.

What does that mean? I'm glad you asked.

The short version is that you want a marketing agency that can do it all, that has a wide spectrum of "weapons" in its arsenal and can employ them as needed.

One approach most definitely does not fit all when marketing window treatment businesses. Different firms have different needs, different budgets, different goals.

They have different levels of competition in their particular areas. Speaking of areas, the geography of a particular window covering business plays a big role in which marketing methods will work best.

For example, paid search engine marketing (SEM) is the most powerful tool for rapidly increasing calls to your window treatment website, but to deliver online traffic over long run, you need to strengthen both your general SEO and specifically your local SEO.

So if you worked with a marketer who only could handle one of these processes, you'd be missing out entirely on the other.

Similarly, some marketers might claim you can gain a lot of customers through their only service — and often that one service is advertising on social media, particularly Facebook.

And yes, that can be a beneficial *component* of a marketing campaign, but it's definitely not the whole ball of wax — no matter what some self-appointed marketing guru claims. At RRM, we help clients with both social media posting and advertising, but that's just one ingredient in the recipe.

Some agencies don't do PPC advertising at all. Some don't do remarketing. Or hyper-geotargeting. Or review and reputation optimization. Or website conversions optimization.

A (frankly shocking) number of agencies are happy to take your money and add your window treatment company to their "one-size-fits-all solution."

And honestly, it doesn't work.

It's also true that you don't want to waste money on marketing services you don't need — or don't fit your particular goals at the time.

A reputable full-stack agency has all the options available, but it *also* won't try to pad its wallet by requiring you to accept a "full suite of services" if some make zero sense for your particular situation.

Instead, a legitimate agency will take the time to understand your exact situation and work *with* you to create a campaign that includes the services with the best ROI and most effectiveness for you.

When scrutinizing a marketing agency, first make sure it effectively employ all the tools listed in this book. Then make sure the agency will *specifically customize a plan* that works best for *you*, employing all the tools *you* need — but none that you don't.

That's how reputable agencies work.

Using an internet marketing pro vs. doing it yourself

In many ways, we now live in a DIY society, and that's a good thing. With the expansion of 24/7 internet access into people's homes, we now have a wealth of information at our fingertips any time of day.

It's like having access to hundreds of thousands of libraries at all times, right there in your office, or living room, or porch, or wherever.

You can take your smartphone to the beach and access 100,000 times more information than a person could at the largest big-city library 25 years ago.

All of that information makes it much easier for people to solve their own problems. Need tips for changing the pedals on your bicycle? There are not only step-by-step guides on the internet, but YouTube videos as well — and they're all completely free.

Some businesses take this approach for their internet marketing efforts. While a few are successful at this, that's generally because the business is related to internet marketing (or something closely affiliated with it) in the first place.

For most brick-and-mortar business owners, the best use of your time is doing what you do well. You should be focused on your clients and your services, not trying to determine which keyword phrase gets you the best PPC results. You should be ensuring that a complicated installation went exactly as planned, not figuring out how to edit image tags in your website code to improve your search engine rankings.

The DIY route might make sense if employing the right internet marketing firm were extremely expensive, but it's not. Some great firms are very affordable, and the increase in business will pay for the initiative many times over.

When it comes to justifying the cost, also consider this: Truly great marketing will help you become more selective.

The more potential clients or customers you have, the choosier you can be. If you only have 10 clients (but can handle 25), you might have to undersell your services, because you can't risk losing the 10 clients you have. However, if 50 people want to use your services, you can set your prices at a much more appropriate rate.

It's good to be selective. At Ring Ring Marketing, quite frankly, *I'm* selective. Virtually every week, I turn down the opportunity to work with several potential clients — people whose money other marketers would gladly take without a second thought.

If the numbers won't work for my business, it doesn't make sense to take on the campaign. (Remember, we have a 100 percent money-back guarantee, so we're taking on all the risk.)

I also turn down a potential client if that business's particular situation means it's unlikely to see a great benefit from our campaigns. I'm not in the business of taking people's money. I'm in the business of helping window treatment businesses grow and succeed. Nothing less is considered a successful partnership to me.

Red flags to watch out for when choosing an internet marketing firm

Now that you know the benefits of hiring a professional to handle your internet marketing, you need to know how to select one. The skills, experience, resources, and customer support abilities of various firms can vary widely from one to another.

Here I'll touch on additional "red flags" that are indicative of the way certain internet marketing consultants, particularly those with large firms, do business. I'll follow each one with a short explanation of how a legitimate business would handle the situation.

RED FLAG #1:

Conflicts of Interest

The problem with many large internet marketing firms is that while they are managing your campaign, they are also managing your direct competitors' campaigns.

You and your window treatment competitors all are competing for presence on the first page of search engine results. The space is limited. Whose interest does the firm have in mind?

In addition, at a big firm, your account representative is hired to sell — not to manage your campaign. How can he manage your campaign if he's pressured by his managers to hit sales goals every week? The rep's incentive is to sell, not to generate more sales for you.

If he triples your sales, he doesn't benefit it any way. If fact, if he ignores your account, he actually makes *more* money, because he's using the time he *should* be helping you to "close" more clients. Your account gets neglected and performance suffers.

At a legit marketing firm, your dedicated account manager is a dedicated marketing professional (at RRM, we call them ***coaches***, because that's a big part of their role), not a salesperson.

The managers are under ***no pressure*** whatsoever to go out and find accounts. Their sole purpose is the continual optimization of your campaign, to bring in customers and make your phone ring.

They have top-level technical expertise in internet marketing and have helped numerous businesses — in particular, window treatment companies — transform leads from online to your phone line.

RED FLAG #2
Lack of transparency

Most companies doing great work want to illustrate what they can achieve. That means sharing all the numbers with their customers. However, many large internet marketing firms do not provide you with all the data associated with your campaigns.

For example, they do not show you what exact keywords they bid on, which match type they use, what the bounce rate is, or the quality score associated with each keyword.

Those terms might be unfamiliar, but they're easily explained by a quality consultant. You don't need to know what all these words mean, but you do need to know that these are the words that measure whether a campaign is actually working.

A good internet marketer will not shy away from providing you a result with all this information. When you do good work for a customer, you want to show it off. You want your customers to know exactly what you're achieving for them. When that information is hidden, you have no way to know.

It's equivalent to FedEx sharing its percentage rates for on-time arrivals. These are the key numbers that measure whether your marketing is succeeding or failing.

At a legit marketing firm, all the data is shared with you. The company should share with you exactly what it has done with your campaign every week. If a company does good work, why would it do anything else?

RED FLAG #3
Retention through contracts, not by results

A number of large internet marketing firms require contracts with minimum term commitments. Why is that a concern? It relates to how internet marketing works.

Business owners generally will know within 2–3 months whether their marketing provider is achieving the results they'd been promised. Unfortunately, if they want to terminate their campaign when they have a minimum term commitment, they're out of luck. Whether the campaign is soaring or nosediving, the business owner is on the hook.

If you're providing real, quantifiable results every month, why require a minimum term?

At a legit marketing firm, programs run month to month. Most partners see results in 30 days, but sometimes it takes 2–3 months, depending on the particular market.

After that time frame, you can terminate the service if you like. However, after 90 days, customers typically are so thrilled with the results that they don't want to leave. They've achieved tremendous growth in their revenue and want to keep that going.

RED FLAG #4
Lack of technical knowledge

A lot of large internet marketing firms do not actually employ internet marketing experts. Instead, they employ (as you'll remember from a few pages back) salespeople. Because *all they care about is sales*.

When you sign on with these firms, the person managing your pay-per-click campaign is not a marketing pro. It's your account representative.

Here's the problem: She's a salesperson, not a marketing technical engineer.

These account reps undergo a few weeks of crash training and are expected to manage your campaign. In fact, they are not certified.

Internet marketing is a very complicated process, and most salespeople are not very good at it. They earn their pay by being good at sales, not internet marketing.

At a legit marketing firm, your dedicated account manager is a dedicated marketing engineer. The managers' sole purpose is to *optimize* your campaign and get your phone ringing with leads for renovation calls.

Unlike larger companies that check in on your account once a week, a legit company will actively manage your account on a daily basis. It will monitor and adjust your campaign every day to achieve the outcome you and the expert decided upon together.

Once the firm has a great pay-per-click campaign set up for you, it can make sure it's always achieving results by working continuously to improve it.

Your target market's keywords might change every month. Your competition might suddenly be paying more for same keywords, lowering your ad position. Perhaps your competition comes up with an ad that has a better offer — your ads still show, but fewer people click on them.

Continuous management is essential to keeping your online advertising costs down. That's what a good firm does.

RED FLAG #5
Focusing on the number of ad clicks, rather than on your business

With many large internet marketing firms, it's in their best interest to drive more clicks and spend all your budget each month, then come back to ask you to spend even more. The company makes its money based on the percentage of your spending.

If that sounds ridiculous to you, well, it does to me too. You're paying good money to drive customers to your website. It is critical that these visitors *go on to call your business*.

These companies do not do any website conversion optimization to ensure that traffic turns into customers. They only care about delivering traffic to your website, not to your phone line.

Here's the problem with that: If your website isn't optimized in the first place — if it has a hard-to-find phone number, no offer, etc. — no amount of traffic will save you.

The primary purpose of the website is to create contact by phone or email. Optimizing your website for this purpose is a vital part of this process.

At a legit marketing firm, it all comes down to the bottom line: delivering a high return on investment. That means turning website visitors into sales.

Conversion rate optimization is an ongoing process of testing and tuning your website to make your phone ring. A good firm teaches you how to fine-tune your site to convert more online visitors into sales.

Conclusions

Staying ahead in a digital world

I've covered a lot of information in this book, and I realize it's a lot to take in.

Even without digging into all the minutiae of various marketing efforts in a digital world, as you can see, it's a very different battlefield than companies dealt with five years ago, or even two years ago.

I could tell you that everything will reach a nice, level plateau for a while, that once you understand how successful business marketing works in a digital world, that you'll be up on the status quo for the next several years.

But that isn't true.

The one constant of successful business marketing today is that nothing is constant. Social media networks that were incredibly influential at the start of this decade (I'm looking at you, MySpace — and you, Friendster) are virtually extinct today.

Mobile phones that were cutting-edge a few years ago can't handle the vast majority of applications that are most used today.

Websites that attracted tons of traffic and converted visitors almost automatically are useless today (if they haven't been updated since then).

It all sounds scary, but in truth, the ever-changing influence of technology on local businesses in this digital age is a very *good* thing — for those willing to adapt and use it to their benefit.

These circumstances provide business owners who can adjust on the fly in 2020 an enormous advantage over local competitors who are still doing business the 2015 way, much less the 2010 way.

I feel fortunate to have worked with lots of great local business owners just like you. I've seen firsthand how much more revenue they can generate by employing the very same tools I cover in this book.

These tools allow small business owners to separate themselves completely from the pack. They can attract and target prospective customers long before their competitors are even aware of them. They can evaluate and measure their marketing approaches on the fly and improve them with virtually no delay.

Yes, things move fast these days. No, it will never be as simple as it used to be to simply run a local business. But that's simply the reality.

Times change, and people who accept that change and adapt to it will thrive. Those who do not, no matter how good they are at what they do, will stagnate and die off.

Perhaps that doesn't seem fair, and that's understandable. If you're the best in your location at providing window covering sales and installation, shouldn't that be all that matters? You do a great job at a fair price. All business should naturally flow to you.

In truth, that's never been the case. Simply being good at your chosen vocation might be enough if you're an employee, but you're not an employee.

You're a business owner. You took the plunge to be enterprising and run your own business, and that's wonderful. And as the owner, you know that whatever you do that running the business side is its own discipline, one that's very different than simply product sales and installation.

That discipline *did* change long before now.

It changed with the advent of websites and email. It changed when payroll went from being calculated with pencils and erasers to Excel spreadsheets. It changed when you went from contacting employees on pagers and walkie-talkies to mobile phones.

Things are just changing faster now. Much, much faster. And it's not just the speed of things — it's also how far their influence has spread demographically. Incredibly powerful technology is in the palm of people's hands, and they're using it. Every age, every race, everywhere.

It doesn't matter if you're in the heart of a big city or working in a small town. Your potential customers are employing this technology in their day-to-day lives, and it's only going to become more pervasive.

This doesn't mean you need to become a master of the digital world. You can run your window covering business and focus on what you do best. I've worked with lots of small business owners who just wanted the phone to ring.

And that's what I do. I employ the techniques in this book, in addition to other methods, as necessary, to attract visitors, to convert those visitors into customers, to make a business's phone ring off the hook.

The business owner can be as involved or removed as he or she likes. Some proprietors want to know and help control every aspect of the process. We can do that.

Some want to be almost entirely hands-off. We can do that too. And anything in between? Never a problem.

That's because you know best how to run your window covering business. You know your strengths and weaknesses. You know what requires your direct supervision and what you can delegate. The same thing works with marketing in the digital world.

You can figure out what works best for you. A qualified marketing expert will adjust to your needs and expectations. The only important thing is making your phone ring.

Having read this book, you might think you need to employ all these marketing aspects immediately. On the other hand, it might sound so overwhelming, you might think it's best to ignore them altogether.

It should be obvious that the second option isn't an option at all. Other small businesses are employing these initiatives. They are getting more bang for their buck, expanding their customer bases, and identifying the best and most profitable customers, using these methods.

With that said, your window treatment company doesn't necessarily need to do everything that's listed here. It depends on what you do. It depends on your budget. It depends on what resources are best directed to provide you the very best return on your investment.

Various marketing companies do things different ways. My company offers a 100 percent money-back guarantee, because we know what we do works. We know how to attract people who are looking for exactly what you provide.

Really, we're just like you: We're good at what we do, and we want to share our expertise with local businesses and help them grow.

Things move fast in the business marketing world, and I don't expect the proprietors I partner with to stay up on these things. That's what *I* handle.

I stay apprised of every twist and turn and use that knowledge to benefit my partners. That's what a good marketing expert should do. It ensures that my clients stay ahead of the game, and it's a game that changes month to month, sometimes week to week.

Now that you've learned the basics of marketing in today's digital world, take some time to assess your marketing efforts and how they've been working for you.

> Do you know how effective your advertising is?

> Do you know what customers are saying about your business online, in user reviews, in ratings, and on social media?

> Do you know whether people can easily access your website on smartphones?

> Do you know whether your business even shows up on Google Maps or Apple Maps?

If you don't know the answer to these questions off the top of your head, it's probably time to take a long look at how you're marketing your business in a digital age.

Business owners who know the answers to these questions are highly visible to potential customers. Those who don't are typically flying way under the radar. You can't afford to be off that radar.

I want to thank you for taking the time to read this book and consider the points I've discussed here. If you're looking for more information on marketing your business in the digital age, I'll be more than happy to speak with you. Here are a few ways to get in touch:

Contact me anytime through email at:
welton@ringringmarketing.com

Visit our website:
ringringmarketing.com

Call us toll-free:
(888) 383-2848

Thanks again, and let me wish you and your business great success now and for many years to come.

Welton Hong

Ring Ring Marketing Information

Ring Ring Marketing only makes money when our clients make money. Our work produces amazing results, so we stand behind it with a <u>60-day no-questions-asked money-back guarantee</u>.

We have a simple evaluation process for businesses interested in partnering with us. We'll discuss your particular company and how we can employ an online marketing campaign structured specifically for you.

Because we specialize in the home improvement industry, we know exactly how to design a campaign we know will be successful for you.

If the numbers don't work out and we're unable to help you, it won't cost you a penny. That's why there's <u>zero risk</u> in contacting us for an evaluation. We want to make it easy for you.

Now is the time to act. You simply can't afford to get left behind. Learn how a professionally executed internet marketing campaign can make this your most successful year ever.

Visit our website:
ringringmarketing.com

Call us toll-free:
(888) 383-2848

Made in the USA
Middletown, DE
20 February 2023

24603565R00125